TAO
MAGIC

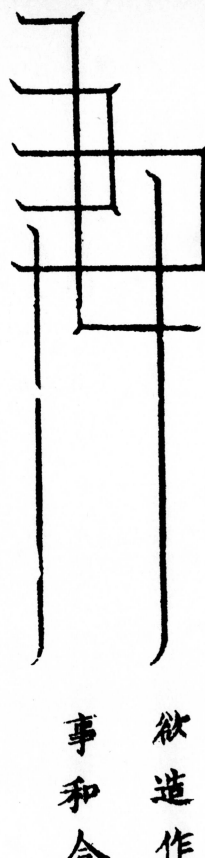

欲造作百事和合吉

LASZLO LEGEZA

TAO MAGIC

*The secret language
of diagrams and calligraphy*

THAMES AND HUDSON

Facing title page:

Talisman for seeking office. In the
performance of all kinds of duties, it will
combine peace with good fortune.
(*Tao-tsang* 668–3:29b)

Printed and bound in Great Britain by
The Alden Press Ltd, Oxford

Contents

Introduction   7

    The Secret Sources   8

    Eternal Change   10

    Vital Breath   13

    Bodily *yin-yang* and Alchemy   15

    The Spirit World   16

    The Magic Power of Calligraphy   18

    The Mystic Graphic Arts   21

    Making Talismans   24

    Talismanic Language   27

    The Taoist Vision   30

The Plates   31

The Figures

    Meditational diagrams and talismans   109

    Charms for summoning spirits   114

    Preventive talismans   116

    Protective talismans   119

    Curative talismans   124

    Implements of magic   125

    Note on the *Tao-tsang* (Taoist canon)   128

    Chronology   128

    Bibliography   128

Introduction

This selection of Taoist magic diagrams, talismans and charms represents an aspect of Chinese art virtually unknown in the West. Art historians – even Eastern art historians – have largely ignored them, concerning themselves primarily with problems of artistic technique rather than meaning, the question of 'how' rather than 'why'. Yet Taoist calligraphy, as I shall be showing, has been of first importance in China since earliest times, both as an artistic carrier of spiritual truths, and as the one means of communication with the spirits.

Taoist graphic art was first and foremost a practical magic, enabling man to communicate with the spirit world and influence the workings of the invisible forces of nature for his own benefit. It was geared to his everyday needs, concerned with the changes of season and weather essential for planting, harvesting, and building. On another level of daily life, the diagrams and talismans were intended to cure sickness, bless marriage, ease childbirth, protect the household from fire, get rid of pestilence and misfortune, guard against calamities. In short, they were to make the daily life of the people easier. Later in the text we shall be looking at the different ways in which these magic diagrams have been made and used, throughout the centuries.

On a deeper philosophical level, the diagrams may be understood as embodying the concepts of Taoist philosophy. They are to help us harmonize the sexual polarities, the *yin* and *yang*, within ourselves, and to place us in harmony with the turbulent energies that act upon our lives and the universe. At the most profound level of all, they point the way to the core of Chinese mysticism. We can intuit the truth that reality is not a succession of separate moments, or an infinite number of separate 'things', but a seamless web of eternal change, like the currents of a river, or clouds blown by the wind; that 'being' and 'non-being' are complementary, just as the fretted stones which we see depicted in the diagrams are given their shape by erosion, and the surrounding silence gives music its form. In the visual arts of China, empty space is as important as line. The final goal of the Taoist mystic is to penetrate beyond ordinary 'reality' to reach to an awareness of

< See p. 114, fig. 21

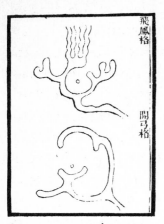

Geomancy patterns known as 'The Flying Male Phoenix' (above) and 'Drawing the Bow' (below). (From Chiang P'ing-chien, *Shui-lung ching* 3:10a. 1744 ed.)

the ultimate tranquillity, that which is beyond time and change, the Great Ultimate, the Whole, the 'mystery beyond all mysteries', called by the Chinese the Tao.

Artistically, the diagrams represent some of the most fascinating examples of Chinese abstract art to develop outside the imperial mainstream, which is what we know as 'Chinese art' today. They are as much a part of the legacy of Chinese art as the celebrated Shang and Chou ritual bronzes and jades, Han and T'ang pottery tomb figurines, Sung academic paintings and calligraphic scrolls, or Ming and Ch'ing dynasty ceramics.

We can see their influence in the symbolic abstraction of these other visual arts. We can also clearly observe their traces in the techniques of various Taoist schools and secret societies which operated all over China from the Han period onwards. These include astrology, palmistry, physiognomy, geomancy, alchemy, herbal medicine, acupuncture, and the arts of movement (t'ai-chi chüan and kung-fu).

The secrecy that has surrounded Taoist teaching arises partly from the taboo on the sacred – the mystic communication has to be protected from the eyes of the uninitiated or irreverent – and partly from the historical need to protect the various cults from official hostility. Even today, talismans have been refused to non-Taoist, non-Chinese enquirers.

The Secret Sources

The present selection of Taoist magic diagrams, talismans and charms has been taken from the most esoteric of the 1,464 works preserved in the *Tao-tsang*, the 1436 (early Ming dynasty) edition of the Taoist canon, and other Ming and Ch'ing dynasty manuals. The *Tao-tsang*, first published about AD 1190, was originally an even larger collection before its burning was ordered by Kublai Khan of the Mongol (Yüan) dynasty in 1281.

In its present (early Ming) form the collection consists of seven different sections ('caves') with various supplements, containing more than fifty million characters of text and several thousand diagrams. Supplementary diagrams were added in the Ming period, but the vast majority of those printed are ancient canonical forms, belonging to a tradition of occult art over two thousand years old, the roots of which go back to shamanistic practices in the second and first millennia BC.

The shaman is a person who has acquired techniques which enable him to contact the spirit world, and, specifically, to summon spirits. His power and prestige largely depend on the number of spirits he can voluntarily incarnate in himself and thereby control. He may be aided by songs, dances, drums and, frequently, narcotics.

There was a limited tradition of these practices in Taoism, particularly in South China, but more frequently Taoist magic used talismans and charms which became impersonal repositories of power. They were impersonal in the sense that, once the talismanic calligraphy had been completed by the Taoist priest, who would usually reproduce a canonical prototype, all his spiritual power was immediately *transferred* to the talisman. It was then used by the individual as a kind of ritual object to retain his direct contact with the spirit.

A profound belief in the spiritual powers of calligraphy was very probably already present even in the formative period of Chinese civilization (i.e. during the first millennium BC), and was largely responsible for the survival of the Chinese ideographic script. For it is significant that, despite several attempts at reform, the Chinese civilization has always shown reluctance to adopt an alphabetic script.

In order to protect the talismanic 'mystery' a number of beautiful secret scripts were evolved by Taoism; how they arose and in what way they differ from ordinary calligraphy, we shall see later in the introduction, when we look at the magic power of calligraphy.

The diagrams as they appear today were the work of a wide range of artists, including illiterate villagers, recluses and hermit-scholars, as well as Taoist exorcist-priests, faith-healers, and sorcerers. Most of them are anonymous, for the powerful talismanic forms are rarely attributed to particular individuals, and the legendary attributions of the Taoist canon must be treated with reservation.

In their original form, these diagrams were the most perishable visual art products of China. Some of these mystic diagrams were originally drawn in the dust with a wooden stick or a finger, others (after Han times) on paper to be burnt as 'paper-money' offerings to the forces of the supernatural. These notes of 'paper-money' were reproduced many thousands of times in the course of a single generation, only to be used for a single day in a given hour of the magic rite. The highly perishable material of which they were made was itself a constant reminder of the cardinal Taoist teaching: the principle of Eternal Change which governs the whole universe. Indeed, most of them have disappeared along with the voices of the famous ancient singers and the movements of celebrated Sui and T'ang dynasty dancers. Yet, they have not been completely lost. Outstanding examples have survived in Taoist canonical sources, and even today are being copied closely. A number are to be found among the illustrations of this book.

Talisman of the Messenger of the Nine Heavens, who can cure epidemics. It depicts a shaman performing a ritual fire-dance. (*Tao-tsang* 1203–224:16b)

Emblem of 'the One', the Great Ultimate (*t'ai-chi*) with interlocking *yin* and *yang* each containing an element of their opposite in the form of a dot. The *yang* half is in the upper position. (Carved jade talisman, early Ming dynasty, probably late 14th or early 15th century. One of the earliest known examples of this symbol used on its own in Taoist art)

figs 11–13

figs 11–13

Eternal Change

At the very root of this occult art we find the ancient Taoist philosophical teachings of *yin-yang*. According to this system, 'the One', the Whole, the Great Ultimate (*t'ai-chi*), produces the negative-positive dualism of *yin* and *yang*, whose continuous interaction gives birth in turn to the Five Elements (*wu-hsing*), from which all events and objects are derived. The principle of *yin* is conceived as sovereign over Earth. It corresponds to negative, female, dark, watery, soft, cold, deadly, still, etc. The principle of *yang* is conceived as sovereign over Heaven. It corresponds to positive, male, light, fiery, hard, warm, living, moving, etc. *Yin* and *yang* divide to form the points of the compass.

The Five Elements, Wood, Fire, Earth, Metal, and Water, like all the cosmos have a *yin* and *yang* aspect. The Ho-t'u, one of the two most ancient Taoist diagrams, is a chart of the Five Elements as they exist in the Prior Heavens of Change in their life-giving, *yang* order. Wood is said to give birth to Fire, Fire to Earth, Earth to Metal, and Metal to Water. Finally, Water gives birth to Wood, and thus starts a new cycle.

During the first part of the year, when nature is on the increase, the *yang* aspect is dominant. During the second half of the year, when nature declines towards winter and death, the *yin* aspect becomes dominant. Thus, in order to accomplish the renewal of the universe, the Ho-t'u diagram alone is not enough. The Taoist must also understand the principles according to which the reverse process from *yang* to *yin* operates. To achieve this, the Taoist uses a second chart called the Lo-shu, the second most ancient diagram, said to have been discovered by the legendary Emperor Yü on the back of a tortoise emerging from the Lo river. The Lo-shu is the diagram of the so-called Posterior Heavens of Change. Here the Five Elements no longer bring life. The creative order of the Five Elements in the Prior Heavens of Change (i.e. Wood, Fire, Earth, Metal, and Water) is rearranged according to the destructive order of the Five Elements in the Posterior Heavens of Change (i.e. Water, Fire, Metal, Wood, and Earth). Thus *yin* Water overcomes *yang* Fire, *yin* Fire destroys *yang* Metal, *yin* Metal destroys Wood, and finally *yin* Wood overcomes Earth. The cosmos must await the rebirth of *yang* and the winter solstice. Men must put the magic Ho-t'u back into the centre of the universe to make nature flourish again and start a new cycle of change.

Like the Ho-t'u, the Lo-shu is basically a diagram of change. According to legend, it inspired King Wen, founder of the Chou dynasty, to create the *Book of Changes* (*I-ching*). It is also a magic square: no matter in which direction the numbers of the Lo-shu are added up, the total is always fifteen.

This Taoist cosmos of eternal change has further implications for occult arts, since the Five Elements are also connected with symbols of direction, colour, season, etc., as set out in the following table, according to their order in the Prior Heavens of Change:

ELEMENT:	Wood →	Fire →	Earth →	Metal →	Water
DIRECTION:	East	South	Centre	West	North
COLOUR:	Blue	Red	Yellow	White	Black
SEASON:	Spring	Summer	Late Summer	Autumn	Winter
NUMBERS AND HEAVENLY STEMS (*yin*)	8, *i*	2, *ting*	10, *chi*	4, *hsin*	6, *kuei*
(*yang*)	3, *chia*	7, *ping*	5, *wu*	9, *keng*	1, *jen*
CLIMATE:	Windy	Hot	Humid	Dry	Cold
MOUNTAINS:	T'ai-shan	Heng-shan (in Hunan)	Sung-shan	Hua-shan	Heng-shan (in Hopei)
PLANETS:	Jupiter	Mars	Saturn	Venus	Mercury
SOUND:	Shouting	Laughing	Singing	Weeping	Groaning
MUSICAL NOTE:	*chüeh*	*chih*	*kung*	*shang*	*yü*
VIRTUES:	Benevolence	Propriety	Faith	Righteousness	Wisdom
EMOTIONS:	Anger	Joy	Sympathy	Grief	Fear
ANIMALS:	Dragon	Phoenix	Ox or Buffalo	Tiger	Snake and/or Tortoise
VISCERA:	Liver	Heart	Spleen	Lungs	Kidneys
ORIFICES:	Eyes	Ears	Mouth	Nose	Anus and Vulva
TISSUES:	Ligaments	Arteries	Muscles	Hair and Skin	Bones
FLAVOUR:	Sour	Bitter	Sweet	Pungent	Salt
ODOUR:	Rancid	Scorched	Fragrant	Rotten	Putrid
EMPERORS:	Fu Hsi	Shen Nung	Huang-ti	Shao-hao	Chüan-hsü
THEIR ASSISTANTS:	Chü Mang	Chu Jung	Hou-t'u	Ju-shou	Hsüan-ming

This doctrine of the Five Elements applies both to the external macrocosm of the universe and to the internal microcosm of the individual self. To a student of the occult, it offers not only a general guide to an understanding of the world but also a means whereby the cosmic pattern of change can be influenced through an act of 'sympathetic magic'. Such an act, however, is much dependent on the precise timing of the change, for which a specialized knowledge of the calendar is necessary.

The normal Chinese calendar is partly lunar, with the length of the month determined by the cycles of the moon, and partly solar, in so far as the length of the year is linked to the four seasons, as in the western calendar. From the point of view of occult practices, however, another calendar system is far more relevant. This is basically a constant repetition of a sixty-year or sixty-day cycle of sixty two-character terms, which has been used in China to designate the element of time since before 1000 BC. A measurement of both days and years, it is formed by revolving a cycle of ten characters, representing the Ten Heavenly Stems, with one of twelve, representing the Twelve Earthly Branches. The ten Heavenly characters are: *chia, i, ping, ting, wu, chi, keng, hsin, jen* and *kuei*. The twelve Earthly characters are: *tzu, ch'ou, yin, mao, ch'en, ssu, wu, wei, shen, yu, hsü* and *hai*. The duodenary system has also been used on its own to designate the twelve months and the twelve double hours of the day, starting at 11 p.m. In addition, there is a number for each person determined by the characters drawn from the cycles marking the year, month, day, and hour of his birth. Taoist occult theory correlates these two sets of characters with the workings of the Five Elements, colours, seasons, etc.

The following passage from the *Pao-p'u tzu*, a Taoist work of about AD 300, explains this concept:

When the *Ling-pao ching* speaks of *protective days*, it means a continuation of the Twelve Earthly Branches and the Ten Heavenly Stems in which the first element begets the second. Days *chia-wu* (no. 31 of the 60-cycle) and *i-ssu* (no. 42) are examples of this. *Chia* is Wood, and *wu* is Fire; *i* too is Wood, and *ssu* Fire, Fire being born of Wood. When it speaks of *proper days*, it means combinations where the second element begets the first. *Jen-shen* (no. 9) and *kuei-yu* (no. 10) are examples of this. *Jen* is Water, and *shen* is Metal; *kuei* is Water, and *yu* is Metal, Water being born of Metal. By *constraining days* it means combinations where the first element conquers the second. *Wu-tzu* (no. 25) and *chi-hai* (no. 36) are examples of this. *Wu* is Earth, and *tzu* is Water; *chi* too is Earth, and *hai* Water, and according to the theory of the Five Elements, Earth conquers Water. By *attacking days* it means combinations where the second element conquers the first; *chia-shen* (no. 21) and *i-yu* (no. 22) are examples of this. *Chia* is Wood, and *shen* is Metal, *i* too is Wood and *yu* Metal, Metal conquers Wood. From these examples one can deduce the rest.

The notes to the talismans which follow contain frequent references to this cyclic system, which is by no means as complicated in its practical application as it appears in the passage quoted above. For example, if a given year, month, day or hour is linked with the element Water, this signifies that a good deal of rain may be expected during the period, while a dominant element of Fire would indicate a hot spell and also an increased risk of fire breaking out. The choice of lucky and unlucky days, which features so prominently in Chinese divination and farmers' almanacs, is only one of the practical extensions of this *yin-yang* and Five Elements theory.

Yin-yang numerical system, as shown in the table above, also played a prominent part in Taoist magic. As we shall see, a large number of talismans were used in sets of threes, fives, nines, etc. 3–5 Among these, the sets of fives were considered particularly powerful 6–10

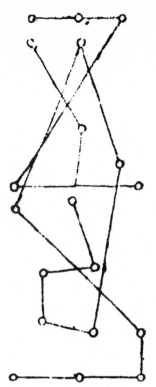

Magic talisman to bring happiness and good fortune, depicting two constellations (*yin* and *yang*) interlocked in acrobatic sexual union. (Early 12th century, *Tao-tsang* 217–25: 2b)

because they acted on the Five-Element space-time factor of the cosmos with associated symbolism of colour, smell, taste, sound, etc. Inspired by the philosophical doctrine of the Five Elements, popular Taoist spiritualism showed itself remarkably practical again: the multiperceptual contact with the spirit world opened up additional channels of communication with the spirits, making use of all the senses of the human body.

Of the heavenly bodies, the radiant Sun represents *yang* and the silver Moon, *yin*. To reinforce *yang*, Taoist magic prescribed sun-bathing in the nude for men, who were instructed to hold a talisman (a secret character for sun written in the *yang* colour, red, on green paper). Moon-bathing in the nude was prescribed for women to reinforce their *yin*, and they too were to hold a talisman (a secret character for the moon written in the *yin* colour, black, on yellow paper). Constellations too, according to the principle of the harmonious (*yin-yang*) unity of heaven and earth, guided and influenced changes on earth. Hence their frequent appearance in talismanic graphic compositions and secret diagrams. They are often represented symbolically as convoluted stones and rock-formations.

Vital Breath

Ch'i, the Vital Spirit, fills the world of the Taoist. It is the Cosmic Spirit which vitalizes and infuses all things, giving energy to man, life to nature, movement to water, growth to plants. It is exhaled by the mountains, where the spirits live, as clouds and mist and, therefore, the undulating movement of clouds, mist, or air filled with smoke rising from burning incense, is a characteristic mystic representation of *ch'i* in Taoist art. As the Universal Force or Eternal Energy, it is at the centre of Taoist breathing exercises, which also involve the art of smelling and the use of incense. In occult diagrams it is the reason for the preference for asymmetrical design. The *Pao-p'u tzu* states: 'Man exists in *ch'i*, and *ch'i* is within man himself. From Heaven and Earth to all kinds of creation, there is nothing which would not require *ch'i* to stay alive. The man who knows how to circulate his *ch'i* maintains his own person and also banishes evils that might harm him.' The same source mentions a method of casting spells by simply rendering breath (*ch'i*) more abundant. The Taoist Chao Ping used to charm streams by breath so that the water-level dropped as much as twenty feet. Using the same technique, he would light a cooking-fire on thatched roofs without setting light to the dwelling, render boiling water harmless for scalding and prevent dogs from barking.

31–4

13

Taoist mystics also conceived of *ch'i* as the invisible underground currents of the earth. Geomancy (*feng-shui* in Chinese, meaning 'wind and water') was born out of this concept. It was concerned with the art of fixing the sites of houses for the living and tombs for the dead in mystic harmony with the local currents of *ch'i*, the Cosmic Energy. Traditionally, if houses and tombs were not correctly sited, evil effects were likely to befall the inhabitants of the houses and the descendants of the dead, whereas a good siting would bring them happiness, prosperity and longevity. The forces and nature of the invisible *ch'i* currents, known also as 'dragon's veins', were determined not only by mountains and hills (*yang*), and valleys and watercourses (*yin*), but also by the movements of the heavenly bodies from hour to hour and day to day all round the year. The *yin* and *yang* aspects of geomancy currents were also identified with the Tiger and the Dragon, which in turn represented the western and eastern quarters of Heaven. As a rule, a three-fifths *yang* and two-fifths *yin* balance was thought to be the most favourable. A magnetic compass marked with trigrams and hexagrams of the *I-ching*, as well as with the sexagenary cycle of stems and branches, aided the complex reckoning for the selection of the suitable site. Compass references have been indicated in the notes on some of the talismans illustrated later in the book.

But *ch'i* also meant sexual energy. The *yin-yang* theory held that the sex organs were a major vehicle of the primary forces of the universe, and looked upon sexual intercourse as an act charged with Cosmic Energy. The schematic symbol of *yin* and *yang* is a circle divided into two equal parts by a curving line, with the lower, or female half dark, and the upper, or male half light. The Earth, woman, and the vulva are all *yin*. Heaven, man, and the penis are all *yang*. The union of these opposites leads symbolically to the harmony of the universe. This also means that it is possible to believe that Heaven and Earth consummate their relation each time a man and a woman perform the sexual act. The prolongation of this act, therefore, becomes a magic ritual. Hence the frequent references, both symbolic and explicit, to the union of the opposite sexes in Taoist magic rites, according to which there were lucky and unlucky days for intercourse, favourable and unfavourable directions and positions in which to lie, etc. There was also an early Taoist ritual known as the 'deliverance from guilt' ceremony which took place on the nights of the new moon and the full moon. It consisted of a ritual dance, the 'coiling of the dragon and playing of the tiger', which ended in successive sexual unions in the assembly. It was censured in a pre-T'ang Buddhist document on the grounds that 'men and women have sexual intercourse in an improper way as they make

Talisman of the Great *Yin*. (Early 12th century, *Tao-tsang* 463–271:28b)

no distinction between nobility and commoners' – a piece of contemporary social criticism which testifies to the egalitarian nature of Chinese Taoist magic.

Bodily yin-yang *and Alchemy*

Man's own body is also governed by the principle of the Great Ultimate (*t'ai-chi*), *yin-yang* and the Five Elements. Traditionally, when *yin* and *yang* were formed out of the primordial chaos, *yang*, being light, went up to form Heaven, while *yin*, being heavy, descended to form the Earth. This idea is repeated in the composition of the human body, with the head as Heaven and the feet as Earth. There is a spirit in each part of the body corresponding to the structure of the universe. The five organs have their ruling spirits, the upper parts of the body contain the *yang* spirits of Heaven, and the lower parts accommmodate the *yin* spirits of Earth. At birth we are filled with the primordial *yang* and, as we grow, this *yang* waxes until, on maturity, it reaches its peak. But *yin* is also present and, as life goes on, *yin* increases and *yang* gradually flows away. When the balance of *yin* and *yang* is no longer effective, we die. Our breath, spirit, and seminal essence are all dissipated. But for the Taoist death is not a separation of the body and spirit as we conceive of it in the West. It is rather a separation of the *yin* and the *yang* elements of man.

Concepts of Taoist internal alchemy also appear in talismanic magic. As we have just seen, the human body was considered to be endowed by Heaven and Earth with the two life-constituents, *yin* and *yang*. They are symbolized by the trigrams *k'an* and *li* respectively. *K'an* and *li* are also the active manifestations of *ch'ien* (representing Heaven) and *k'un* (representing Earth), thus symbolizing their influences. In alchemical terms, *ch'ien* and *k'un* also represent the furnace (the 'subtle fire' of the body) and the crucible (the centres in the body where energy is transformed), while *k'an* and *li* are the ingredients combining in the crucible to form the elixir of life. Trigrams *k'an* and *li* also stand for the sacred union of *ch'ien* and *k'un*, and that of *yin* and *yang*. This union is said to be the magic union of the solar and lunar influences, for in the *I-ching*, *k'an* and *li* represent the moon and sun.

These were the chief principles governing Taoist thinking, and the main purpose of the magic rites and ritual activities of popular Taoism, with its use of talismans and charms, was to win the blessing associated with *yang* and suppress the dark forces of *yin*.

Finally, in accordance with the ancient principle of Taoist inner alchemy, certain post-Han Taoist cults stressed the idea of giving

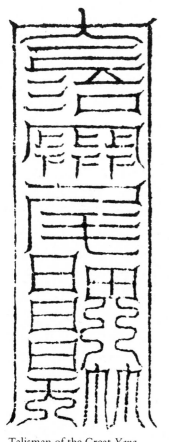

Talisman of the Great *Yang*. (Early 12th century, *Tao-tsang* 463–271:28a)

15

Talisman of the Ruler of the South, to assist in refining spiritual energy, and by Taoist Inner Alchemy, to achieve immortality. The design incorporates a gourd-shaped crucible with *lien* – 'to smelt' or 'to refine' – beneath. (*Tao-tsang* 1152–29:6b)

birth to a new man within oneself, instead of producing offspring externally. This 'infant' represented the immortal soul which was finally externalized when the soul left the mortal body and joined the spirit world. This inward concentration of life-forces, aided by talismanic magic, is symbolized by the image of the flaming 'pearl,' a frequent talismanic graphic component, representing the offspring of the union of *k'an* and *li*, the human and cosmic Energies enveloped in the fire of transformation.

The Spirit World

During the centuries of the Han and post-Han periods (i.e. from the second century BC onwards), popular Taoism began to develop a large pantheon of the spirit world which numbered tens of thousands by the end of the Ch'ing period. Both zoomorphic and anthropomorphic images, representing gods, spirits and demons, appear in this pantheon. They are drawn from ancient Chinese nature-worship, local hero-cults and ancestor-worship, and are so numerous that it would be impossible to list them all. The gods are divided into two categories: those of the Prior Heavens, and those of the Posterior Heavens. At the top of the hierarchy are the gods of the constellations, i.e. the Prior Heavens, the abode of the transcendent and eternal Tao. The Prior Heavens are exempt from changes and represent the mystic sources of life, primordial breath, and blessing in the world of the Posterior Heavens. The gods commonly worshipped by Taoists as patron spirits are those of the Posterior Heavens, where change does take place. They are divided into three groups: those of the Heaven, those of the world of nature and man, and those of the underworld hidden beneath the oceans. These three sections of the visible world are governed by the change of seasons and the continuously revolving complementary interaction of *yin* and *yang*.

The highest of the Taoist divinities are the Three Pure Ones of the Prior Heavens. These are the so-called Primordial Heavenly Worthy, Elder Lord of the Heaven, controlling the past; the Precious Spiritual Heavenly Worthy, Ling-pao, Lord of the Earth, also known as the Jade Emperor, controlling the present; and the Precious Divine Heavenly Worthy, Tao-te, Lord of Man, also known as Lord Lao, controlling the future. They reside in the three highest of the heavenly realms. The Three Pure Ones, lords of Heaven, Earth and Man are also lords of the head, the chest and the belly in man, corresponding also to primordial breath, spirit, and seminal essence.

Of even greater antiquity than the Three Pure Ones are the Five

Primordial Spirits, who also dwell in the Prior Heavens, but are summoned to Earth during rituals. These are the five spirit-emperors: Fu Hsi for the East, Shen Nung for the South, Huang-ti for the Centre, Shao-hao for the West, and Chüan-hsü for the North. They are accompanied by their assistants or spirit-ministers, and are closely connected with the workings of *yin-yang* and the Five Elements, as well as with the animals and star-spirits symbolizing the Five Directions. The five great mountain peaks of China are considered to be the special repositories of these spirits of the Five Directions, and are thus symbolically treated as sources of the Five Elements. For example, Hua-shan is the dwelling place of the spirits in the west, and the source of Metal.

All other spirits who rule the visible world (like the Three Star-gods of Happiness, Prosperity and Longevity, or the Kitchen God) watch over men's good and evil deeds and report them to the heavenly rulers for reward or punishment. In popular Taoism, the highest spirits commanding *yang* influences are resident in Heaven and provide life and blessing. The demons of the underworld are the spirits of men who have died violent deaths or committed suicide, or orphan souls lacking ancestor's tablet or offspring. These bring misfortune, sickness and calamity to mankind. Good spirits, on the other hand, are invariably those of virtuous men and women who worked on behalf of mankind (e.g. as healers) during their lives, and who have become local cult figures after death so that their power and good influence should continue to operate. But in this Taoist spirit world 'bribery' exists as well as the power of accumulated 'merit': demons and spirits were symbolically given talismanic 'paper money', just as the mandarins of imperial China were offered bribes in return for their favour or influence. Clearly this is an indication of the effect of China's mandarin society on the Taoist system – the use of burnt offerings to spirits predates the use of actual paper money by over two thousand years. As a rule, gods worshipped at seasonal festivals and rites were only summoned at other times in the case of great disasters or calamities.

In folk religion and in magic rites contact was primarily with the lower level of the spirit world: the *shen* spirits and the *kuei* demons. According to *yin-yang* theory, before death the *yang* part of a man's soul is *hun*, and after death, it is *shen*. The *yin* part of the soul before death is *p'o*, and after death, it is *kuei*. Thus the *yin* part of the soul after death is usually associated with demons and evil. The *kuei* may also be the harmful spirit of a man who has not been properly returned to earth in burial; a person, for instance, who has died by drowning. In

6–10

18

many cases, people who have died violent deaths have *kuei* and not *shen* spirits. In Chinese mythology, they appear to seek vengeance on mankind for their unfortunate position. In some parts of China, however, they are regarded as patrons of gamblers and prostitutes.

According to Taoist beliefs, the *yin* soul is divided into seven and is connected with the emotions, while the *yang* soul is divided into three and is responsible for human virtues. These emotions and virtues also correspond to the Five Elements, Seasons, Directions, etc., as shown in the chart above (*p. 11*). Thus man's relation to this many-layered spirit world of the popular Taoist pantheon, which already numbered several hundred in Han times, was further complicated by the contribution of later Taoist teachings, mostly of sectarian nature, in the fields of geomancy, alchemy, medicine, etc. As a result, the Taoist vocabulary of the period acquired fresh connotations, and the visual arts developed new dimensions of occult symbolism. These included the esoteric significance of the unity of the round Heaven and the *fig. 4* square Earth; nature worship, from sacred mountains to indoor dwarf plants; the intentionally vague concept of *ch'i*, Cosmic Energy, and its careful preservation in the body through Taoist self-cultivation, breathing exercises and prolonged sexual intercourse. Thus the vocabulary of Taoist occult art was founded on the concept of multiperceptual communication with the spirit forces of the universe, from which grew the notion that the arts should appeal simultaneously to sight, hearing, taste and feel, and should include movement, a principle alien to Western art traditions, in which any particular art is expected to appeal to two of the senses simultaneously at most.

The Magic Power of Calligraphy

The magic power of talismans derived, as we have seen, from the fact that, according to Taoist belief, they were *permanently* inhabited by spirits. Thus men were able to communicate directly with spirits by means of these talismans without the participation of a medium. The talismans themselves acted as mediums, and were to be treated with the greatest respect, veneration, and secrecy. The interdependence of the Taoist spirit world with the material world made the use of talismans much more significant than it would be to Western spiritualists, since spirits were believed to play a commanding role throughout the whole universe, and not merely in a realm of ghosts and supernatural beings. Moreover, talismans constituted the basic essentials for individual Taoist religious practice and worship, as well as for communal rites.

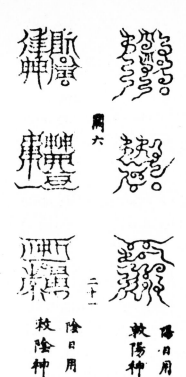

Talismans for Summoning Spirits by Ornamental Beauty, to be written on blue paper in red, and burnt as offerings. The set of three in rounded (*yin*) style of calligraphy (on the right) are to be used 'on *yang* day(s) to have intercourse with the *Yang* Spirits'. The set of three in the squarish (*yang*) style of calligraphy (on the left) are to be used 'on *yin* day(s) to have intercourse with the *Yin* Spirits'. (*Tao-tsang* 221–1:26a)

Spoken charms and spells predated written and painted talismans in China as in other parts of the world. The composition of the Chinese character *shou*, meaning 'invocation of spirits', shows two 'mouth' graphs at the top and a magic wand underneath, strongly suggesting the participation of two people, one presumably a medium, engaged in the task of invoking the spirits. Under shamanistic influence, mediums seem to have played a very significant part in the mystic experiences of Chinese Taoists during the Han period and before. And talismans of particular power were believed to have been composed by those Taoist mystics who were able to communicate directly with the spirits.

Contemporary Han and post-Han sources invariably emphasize the unusual graphology of protective charms and spells received by the mystics from the spirits. They refer to various 'cloud scripts', archaic script forms, and commonly unrecognizable forms of script and graphic compositions charged with magic power which were secretly handed down by the early Taoist mystics. Some of these were written on peach-wood plaques, such as the Weapon-Averter seal talismans of the Chou period, measuring 6 by 3 inches, written in five colours, and placed on gates and doors during the month of midsummer. Others, like the post-Han Five-Colour Talisman, which guarded against pestilence and all kinds of illness, were inscribed on paper or silk of various colours. Yet others were written on gold or jade tablets. In addition to black ink, red cinnabar was used for the calligraphy. The Red Spirit Talisman, for instance, which was worn on the body primarily to guard against death or wounding in battle, consisted of drawing in red cinnabar on vertical strips of yellow paper.

The size of the written character or characters varied considerably: some, like the Enter-Mountain Amulets attributed to Lao-chün to protect travellers in mountainous regions, were inscribed in specially large characters to fill the whole oblong plaque or paper strip. Others only had one or two characters written on them: the 'Emperor of the North', for instance, which afforded protection against crocodiles and insects, as well as winds and waves. Some combined a word of command or request with semi-abstract representations of spirit mountains, constellations, or elements of thunder and lightning (to frighten demons). Others consisted of amulets about two inches square, carved from the pith of jujube and inscribed only with archaic seal-script characters: the Lao Tan Amulet, for example, which protected against tigers, i.e. symbolically against the influence of the *yin* (female) element. More commonly, however, the talismans were oblong strips with written characters descending in a single or combined vertical form, rather than spreading horizontally. The strong esoteric influence of this strip-format is indicated by the fact that it has survived intact in the format of both Chinese and Japanese hanging paintings, particularly landscapes, in later centuries.

Originating from, and inhabited by spirits, these compositions were treated with the utmost reverence. To receive their favour, one had to perform a brief personal introduction to them by name, bow to them at least twice and, if necessary, pronounce the prescribed incantation. When this ceremony had been performed, the talismans would be placed in garments, on doors or gates, or burned to provide protection. In the latter case, the ashes might or might not be consumed, according to the prescribed ritual. Although the talisman was traditionally produced for the layman by an initiated Taoist priest, the priest was not required, except in the case of specially prescribed cures or exorcism, to communicate with the spirit world. On the other hand, certain highly powerful talismanic formulae were transmitted by Taoist mystics from generation to generation in utmost secrecy. Many of the examples illustrated in this book belong to this class.

In a description of the contemporary use of talismans, the *Pao-p'u tzu* (*c.* AD 300) lists several forms much used at the time. Among these were some to be written in red cinnabar and worn by travellers in mountains and forests; others to be fastened on doors, corners, pillars and beams, and set up at important road-junctions and public spots; others 'to reduce to subjection'; and finally, the Charm of Universal Peace attributed to the founding figure of philosophical Taoism, Lao-tzu (sixth century BC).

The uninitiated were of course unable to read these talismans and charms. The *Pao-p'u tzu* complains that no layman could detect the errors in them although some were suspect, and various Taoist sources of later centuries ascribed the inefficacity of talismans to the use of mutilated versions or faulty copies. The increasing use of calligraphic magic talismans by the fifth century could not prevent the decline of old talismanic graphic traditions: indeed, it opened avenues for fresh visual interpretations, culminating in the flowering of Taoist art of the Sung period.

Magic diagrams, talismans and charms required a secret language for their expression, a symbolism outside the scope of the ordinary graphic vocabulary of Chinese writing and painting. For this purpose, popular Taoism was able to draw upon the unlimited resources of the Chinese inventive genius. But in order to find unorthodox calligraphic expression, or to modify existing forms for occult use, the artist had to

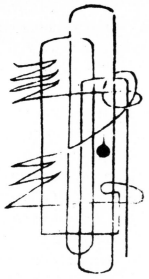

Talisman to bring assistance from the Supreme Jade Sovereign. In red on white paper, to be burned with an incantation of 36 characters. (*Tao-tsang* 1152–34:2b)

solve an almost insuperable problem. The rules governing the use of the sensitive Chinese writing brush, one of the most ingenious inventions of Chinese civilization, were rather inflexible. Strictly speaking, there was only one way of writing a Chinese character correctly. The rules of the brush were admittedly more flexible for painting and for the so-called 'free' calligraphic exercises, in which the character was sometimes modified out of recognition. To fulfil his function, the occult artist had to stay either partly or completely outside the traditional conventions of Chinese calligraphy which, for example, did not accommodate waves and curving lines, or circular forms in script. Hence the emphasis on these in 'free' calligraphic exercises. Sometimes, of course, the writer was an illiterate folk-artist, and therefore already outside the tradition, so that his contribution to the vocabulary of unorthodox expression was fortuitously non-conformist.

The Mystic Graphic Arts

Taoist philosophy has been called at the same time scientific and mystical. And this applies equally to the magic art of Taoist talismanic composition. But the graphic styles of the diagrams clearly reveal two categories of inspiration: some display an acquaintance with brushed calligraphy, or incorporate elements of it; others simply do not show any relation to, or influence from, the conventional technique. In the second category we find imitations of wood-carving and needle-work techniques at one end of the spectrum, and, at the other, the blood-stained impressions left upon the paper by the cut tongue of the medium. These bloody marks represent the words of the spirit, and the utterances of spells by the medium. It is also an example of the creation of new talismans by means of the mediumistic practices of the Spirit Cloud (*shen-hsiao*) Sect of Taoism, which dates back to the Hsüan-ho reign period (AD 1119–26) of the Northern Sung dynasty. These practices have survived until the present day in Hong Kong and Taiwan. M. Saso, in his *Taoism and the Rite of Cosmic Renewal*, has an illustration of a half-naked medium cutting himself with a sword while in trance, and carrying on his back a talisman dipped in blood.

The variety of occult graphic compositions is enormous, ranging from the spontaneity of trance-drawings to the meticulous draughtsmanship of pseudo-scientific diagrams and magic charts. However, the technique of execution remains uniformly unsophisticated, lacking the subtle texture strokes of academic painters. But the Northern Sung School and the School of Literati (*wen-jen*) of the Yüan period accepted some of the principles inherent in Taoist graphic art, together with its mystic values, and thus from the Sung period onwards, inspired calligraphers and painters were generally regarded as people able to communicate with the spirits. As a result, the spiritual cult of calligraphy (and painting) long venerated by Taoists, became firmly established beyond the boundaries of talismanic graphics.

Furthermore, talismanic calligraphy included other means of symbolic contacts with the powers of the supernatural: first and foremost, the elements of magic dance. As an art of movement, dance symbolized the principle of change. The magic dance of the legendary limping Emperor Yü is often referred to in talismanic compositions. These movements which were taught to Yü by heavenly spirits to give him command over the spirits of nature, originally represented a kind of hopping dance that Taoist shaman sorcerers often performed while in trance. But the Taoists were primarily concerned with the magic power of calligraphy, and considered its effectiveness to lie above all in the line traced by the

fig. 18   sorcerer's feet in dance, a line which reproduces a vortex, a spiral of magic, frequently reinforced by constellations.

What are the chief merits of this Taoist graphic art?

First of all, we find that it provided the foundation for a high level of abstraction in Chinese art as a whole, creating forms of a primarily graphic nature for the basic concepts of Taoist teachings, which were metaphysical, rather than ethical, embodying such concepts as Change, Movement, and Energy. Ancient China's lack of epic traditions ensured a fertile soil for this abstract symbolism. It penetrated artistic life beyond the visual, influencing the arts of movement, for instance, and music. As Taoist graphic art recognized no lines of demarcation between the real and the imaginary, it could appeal equally to all, from the philosophically minded to the least sophisticated, although at very different levels. The active use of the imagination in interpreting abstraction was the cardinal point in this type of Taoist art, and still survives in many areas of Chinese art and literature. In traditional Chinese opera, for instance, the almost bare stage is traditionally filled in by the imagination of the spectator.

In addition, Taoist occult artists developed the basic grammar of a superbly rich artistic language designed to symbolize and embody continuity of form (i.e. material reality) in space (i.e. imagination). Through observation of rolling clouds and mist, undulating waves, rising vapour and smoke – the most intangible of all phenomena – they established linear representations for Change, Movement, and Energy. The basic grammar of this artistic language constituted a unique form

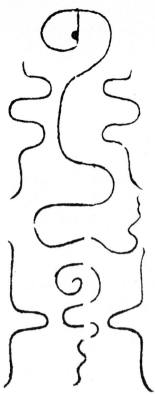

Talisman for purifying the body, to be burned with an incantation of 37 characters which can be rendered as follows: 'The Spirit of Uncleanness is already dissipated, exhausted in the three places to be guarded [i.e. ears, eyes and mouth]. The turbid torrent has been cleansed by the Golden Tower and the Illuminated Royal Apartments. Go high above to contact the Primordial Lord, the Twenty-four True Ones, all in the form of Divine Spirits, to ascend mysteriously from the darkness. Without delay, as the True Order commands.' (*Tao-tsang* 217–30: 22a)

39,40

of rhythmic linearity, uniting the perceptible – the pulse beat of the human body – with the invisible ether of breath and spirits. This Taoist-inspired abstract linearity is already to be seen in the decorative arts of the late Chou period: in bronzes during the sixth and third centuries BC; in the lacquer of the Chang-sha type of the third century BC; and in silk and painted pottery designs of the Han period.

Curving lines which at first allowed man to contact the spirit world, later took on the opposite function in popular occult art: namely they were the one way to outwit evil spirits who can move only in a straight line!

This graphic art of the occult also helped, in a typically Taoist fashion, to establish the significance of 'no statement' which enables one to make a statement. It created the mystic as well as the artistic framework to blend 'statement' with calligraphic 'emptiness' in the true complementary manner of the magic interaction of *yin* and *yang*. Thus 'emptiness', or 'no statement', becomes a statement in this art; a mystic statement, skillfully representing the elements of uncertainty in real life, the vagueness of destiny, or the obscurity of the future. The musical pause, the momentary stillness in dance, or the enclosed emptiness in calligraphic composition or painting, all become an inseparable part of the whole, just as the negative *yin* or the positive *yang* alone cannot form a complete interlocking symbol of the two, representing the Great Ultimate.

Taoist graphic art also produced a system of symbolic multiplicity which went well beyond the ordinary limits of the visual arts. This repertoire of symbolism had a metaphysical significance which was applied alike to Heaven, Earth, and mankind. It sought to unite men and spirits into a single state in emulation of the perfect harmony of *yin* and *yang*, or of Heaven and Earth. Thus we find that the cavities of rock-formations also symbolize stars, which in turn represent lanterns. Similarly, the footpath marked out on the Taoist pilgrim's guide-map to the sacred mountains becomes a magic line on the chart to find the spirits. On another level, the 'sound' of blue jade lends its 'colour' to the sky, and phallic diagrams become 'Heavenly Cures'. To make matters still more complicated, the world of imperial China was also incorporated into the Taoist system when, for example, the term for summoning spirits, 'induce to come', took on the additional mandarin meaning: 'by imperial order'.

The Taoist practice of using intimidatingly vivid colours, however, was never taken up by the academicians of Chinese fine art. Such colours, which were also used in the related art of paper-cuts, directly reflected the colour consciousness of the *yin-yang* world of symbolism, besides expressing the inherent desire of the Taoist occult to create a different art, suitable for communication with the spirits. Talismanic colours and colour-combinations – characteristically Chinese reds, yellows, greens, and blues – contributed to the splendour of popular *fig. 66* Taoist festivals in the decoration of streamers, banners, kites, lanterns, brooms, baskets, parasols and fans, all of which were employed in Taoist magic rites. Of these, brooms were traditionally regarded by the shamans as magic implements to sweep away evil spirits. The long shapes of the streamers and strip-banners indicated talismans with their inscriptions and symbolic designs. And their movements in the wind, which would cause them to show or hide their inscriptions or designs with each gust, symbolized the uncertainty and suddenness of man's contact with the spirits. Similarly, the flash of the ancient bronze mirrors, which was supposed to signify lightning and thunder, also represented this moment of spiritual contact, although these magic phenomena were later reinterpreted according to popular occult tradition as no more than functions of exorcism. Some Taoist sects, however, remained very much aware of the concept of the momentary spiritual experience, vision, insight or inspiration, and brought it into the foreground to meet the challenge of Ch'an (Zen) Buddhism in Sung times. Occult Taoism nevertheless did not prove sufficiently flexible to make much of the Buddhist concept of Enlightenment: its followers turned instead to the world of metamorphosis familiar to the West in the form of Chinese ghost stories, and placed increasing emphasis on the concept of immortality.

To return to the ritual objects used in Taoist popular festivals and communal rites, the flickering lights (*yang* element) of lanterns were to guide the spirits to the altars during seasonal rites at night (the *yin* period). The colourful parasols provided shade (*yin* element) against the burning sun, thus regulating its *yang* influence. The movement of fans brought currents of *ch'i*, Vital Energy; while baskets of flowers provided the various scents – another *yin-yang* 'regulator' in man's communication with the spirit world. Spoken charms, spells, and chants combined with talismans to give multiperceptual contacts with the spirits over and above the visual art of calligraphy.

Making Talismans

In order to assess the early popular Taoist concept of talismans, one should note that the Chinese word for talisman, *fu*, originally designated written tallies or contracts. In Han times, talismanic charms attributed to the inventor of magic charms, Chang Tao-ling (first

Consultation of a magic diagram. (Early 17th-century illustration from the *Shui-hu ch'üan t'u*)

Consultation of the magic formations of yarrow sticks. (Early 17th-century illustration from the *Shui-hu ch'üan t'u*)

century AD), also known as Chang T'ien-shih or Heavenly Master Chang, the legendary founder of the Heavenly Master Sect, represented a kind of contract made with the spirits. As such, they were looked upon as important documents of contract to be carried on the body to provide permanent protection. They guaranteed command over the spirits whenever it might be required. This popular Taoist belief, indeed, prevailed alongside the more profound mysticism of philosophical Taoism for centuries. The use of 'protective contract' talismans appears to have been universal, but popular Taoism favoured the use of specific talismans as well. In fact, the ever-increasing variety of printed talismans from the Sung period onwards proves their immense popularity. Even up to the present day, an estimated two million talismanic New Year prints are marketed in China annually.

There are over three thousand basic talismans preserved in the monumental compendium of the Taoist canon, with several hundred other magic diagrams and charts. These examples provide ample material to enable us to analyse the art of making talismans as well as their underlying graphic principles.

As we have seen, the use of talismans was governed by the *yin-yang* Five Elements theory, the complex doctrine which taught that men were able to influence the processes of the universe by their *participation* through magic (as opposed to the teaching of religious acceptance of Confucianism and, to a large extent, Buddhism). In the course of the centuries following the Han period, this system acquired lavish accretions from folk art and festivals, to such an extent that, by the seventeenth and eighteenth centuries, it became practically impossible for the uninitiated to observe the outward signs of it correctly. In fact, outsiders were hardly aware of the complex esoteric preparations which preceded the performance of Taoist occult rites. Only recently have reliable accounts been published for the first time. These provide fascinating information on the precise timing of Taoist occult rites, including the making of talismans. For example, after the day and hour of the ceremony had been determined by an astrologer in accordance with the temple's geomancy and the nature of the festival, a list was drawn up of those people whose presence would be inauspicious to the occasion. This was because their eight characters (i.e. the cyclic double characters for year, month, day, and hour of birth) would clash with the elements governing the auspiciousness of the chosen day. In fact, their presence would not only be an expression of disrespect, it might also incur the actual hostility of the spirits.

In talisman-making, the timing was equally important. Talismans of Chung Kuei, for example, the popular devil-catcher whose cult

75

goes back to T'ang times, had to be composed not only on the day of his festival – the Fifth Day of the Fifth Moon – but preferably during the *wu* hour of that day, i.e. between 11 a.m. and 1 p.m.

Among a host of similar examples we may single out the practice of making medicinal talismans by Taoist doctors (known as *chu-yu-ko*). The treatment of an illness included chanting the name of a particular healing spirit while tracing the charm or talisman on paper. The ashes of this paper, mixed with the appropriate 'carrier' drug, was believed to be efficacious whether swallowed or used externally. The doctor had to be familiar with the spirits of all the thirteen branches of Taoist medicine (namely, the greater veins, winds, arrestives, external infections, swellings, mouth and teeth, eyes, ears and nose, obstetrics, external injuries, external wounds caused by metal weapons, acupuncture, and pediatrics), as well as their related diseases, principal curative areas, and appropriate charms. In addition, he was required to observe specific geomantic codes for establishing his surgery. This had to be spacious and far away from the kitchen and living quarters of the house. In the centre stood the altar for the spirit of the Yellow Emperor with his image hanging above it. To the left was a second altar for healing spirits, whose names were written in ink on red paper, and to the right was the altar of Lao-tzu. Before all three were containers with offerings of ripe fruit and flowers. The most important feature, however, was a low square table specially installed to hold the implements necessary for writing charms. On it would be laid out secret Taoist talismanic writings, papers of various colours, brushes, cinnabar, ink, and clean water.

The procedure in the treatment of the sick was as follows: after the patient had told the Taoist doctor his symptoms, he was led to the image of the Yellow Emperor where he (or his representatives) burnt incense and bowed formally four times. The doctor then recited the water incantation, the cinnabar incantation, the ink incantation, the brush incantation, the paper incantation, the incantation for writing the selected charm and, finally, the incantation to summon the spirits of the appropriate branches of Taoist medicine involved in the case. After this, the doctor painted the charm, at the same time silently repeating the Yellow Emperor's chant for healing. When he had finished, he wrote the two characters *chih ling*, meaning 'induced to come' or 'by imperial order', on the top of the paper and placed it on the altar. Then having sprinkled three drops of water on the 'Summon the Spirits' charm, he took a mouthful of water and sprayed it over the talisman he had just painted. After making the healing spirit incantation, he rose, clicked his teeth three times to mark a pause, bowed

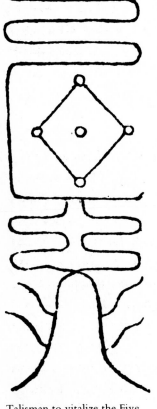

Talisman to vitalize the Five Viscera. (13th century, *Tao-tsang* 1204–42: 31a)

Talisman to prolong life. (Early 12th century, *Tao-tsang* 463–271 : 27b)

formally, picked up the talisman and retired. Finally, he wrapped the talisman in white paper and gave it to the patient with instructions on how to burn it (i.e. how to send it to the spirits) and what additional drugs to take. The patient would then take the talisman home in his left (*yang*) hand.

Equally elaborate was the procedure for making the magic peach-wood wands used in trance-drawings. In this type of talismanic composition (more often found in South China), the drawing was traced on a thin layer of sand or rice spread on a table. The medium sometimes took the wand in both hands or, alternatively, allowed one hand to be held by a person wanting to establish contact with the spirits and record the talismanic message. The drawing might later be transferred to paper, particularly if the diagram was proved to be sufficiently powerful. The peach-wood was usually cut from a twig growing on the east side of the tree, since the peach was associated with the immortal paradise of the Queen Mother of the West, and this arrangement therefore symbolized the union of East and West. On the side opposite the twig, characters meaning 'Spirit of the Clouds' (*yin*) would be cut in the bark of the tree. As implements of automatic writing, these wands were regarded as especially powerful and were frequently used in exorcism, as were peach-wood calligraphic swords. According to popular Taoist belief, the instruments used for writing talismans and charms were themselves so powerful that they were capable of defeating not only ghosts and evil spirits, but also hostile animals and men.

Talismanic Language

Five basic colours were traditionally used in paper charms and talismans for, since spirits moved in all five directions, a suitable colour or combination of colours was needed to control them. Yellow represented the Centre, blue the East, red the South, white the West, and black the North. Of these, red was especially important in that it also symbolized blood, the life-force, and was considered to have supreme magic power. Red talismanic paper protected the whole family from pestilence and ills. The belief that red brought good fortune and long life is indicated by the extensive use of red cinnabar in Taoist alchemy in perpetual search for the elixir of life. The prevalence of cinnabar-red carved lacquers in popular Taoist magic art can also be linked to the magic powers of red, since they are frequently adorned with benevolent talismanic inscriptions. In view of the auspicious meaning of red, it is easy to understand the popular appeal of this colour when it

Exorcist charm to be used against the noxious influences of the Black Tiger of the Mountains and the Black Fog. (*Tao-tsang* 1152–37:2b)

Talisman to protect the body, composed of the character *sheng* – 'life'. (*Tao-tsang* 1203–226:3a)

became the symbol of a political movement in China, as was the case with the Chinese Communist Party. Again, one can better understand Red Guard demands in recent years that red should be the 'Go' colour at traffic lights, instead of green.

The widespread Chinese superstition about destroying any kind of paper is certainly connected with the talismanic use of paper in Taoist occult practices. For paper has always been a relatively cheap and easily available material in all parts of China.

Talismanic language required, first and foremost, a visual statement of the unity of Heaven above and Earth below, and this was expressed in the verticality of the composition, whatever the differences of detail. In early Taoist symbolism, thin lines represented Heaven and thick lines Earth. In later centuries, a rounded style of calligraphy was used to indicate *yin*, no doubt deriving from the clouds which represented that aspect. On the other hand, a squarish style of calligraphy indicated *yang*, referring presumably to hard, angular rock-formations. Therefore, the ancient Chinese symbolism of the round Heaven and square Earth did not apply to talismanic graphics. On the contrary, the rounded, soft style was *yin*, the hard, squarish style, *yang*.

Dots, either connected by straight lines or not, represented stars and constellations. In combined compositions, these appear in the upper, celestial half of the talisman. Such visual references to the stars are frequently to be found in charms against demons, for celestial deities were powerful destroyers of spectres as well as dispensers of felicity. Hence, too, the visual reference to constellations in terms of cavities of rock-formations, re-emphasizing the unity of Heaven and Earth. In other instances, constellation dots outline human figures and convey a bizarre, almost futuristic mood of expression, as we can see in the Armour of Man talisman of Sung or Yüan date, where the image is strangely reminiscent of a twentieth-century spaceman.

Ascending and descending lines found in various types of talismanic calligraphy are another reference to the invisible lines of contact between celestial spirits above and terrestrial beings below. This concept of linear contact is very close to the shamanistic symbol of the Tree (*axis mundi*) which was said to be the home of the spirits permitting ascent to the various heavens or descent to our world. The lines occur with surprising regularity in all kinds of talismans. When broken, they resemble the shape of the Chinese character for 'bow', and this has resulted in another false interpretation by the uninitiated of later centuries, who taught that the character had been incorporated into the talismans because the bow was a weapon especially feared by evil spirits.

The vortex, or spiral of the ancient Taoist Cosmic Energy, which is the dominant sign of the celestial upper half of the talismanic compositions in some of the most ancient charms preserved in the *Pao-p'u tzu*, was later believed to symbolize thunder and lightning – a result of the growing influence of a great variety of thunder-and-lightning gods invented by popular Taoism in post-Han times.

Since talismans and charms were believed to produce whatever condition they expressed, Taoists invented a great variety of them, in particular, characters which express the blessings of *shou* (longevity), and *fu* (happiness). Archaic and fanciful talismanic representations were produced for them in a hundred different forms, and used by way of decoration on all sorts of objects from lacquer to silk embroidery. Written characters denoting felicity, and therefore producing it, likewise appeared regularly in charms on the grounds that they frustrated evil. Talismans also contained threats and commands directed at evil spirits. Among these, we find the character *sha* (to murder) with great regularity. Another powerful character for charm-writing is *cheng*, which denotes the Order of the Universe, before which all evil influences must disappear. It is frequently accompanied by *chih*, also meaning 'order', so that the charm enjoins good behaviour on evil spirits in accordance with the Order. By no means less powerful and frequent are the characters for Sun and Moon, which are often combined to form the character *ming*, meaning light – a devil-destroying power with *huo*, fire.

A very prominent position in talismanic graphics was held by *ting*, the fourth of the ten Heavenly characters, which represents South and, therefore, the devil-destroying element of Fire. In the sexagenary cycle *ting* recurs six times to perform its exorcising function, hence *ting* is written six times in some talismans. A similar part is played by *chia*, the first of the ten Heavenly characters, which represent East where the devil-destroying Sun rises.

Talismans were of course inscribed with the names of benefactor and protector spirits. But even more extensive was the use of the rough drawings supposed to be portraits of gods. Frequently in fragmentary form, with only an arm or leg indicated, their magic effect was regarded as even stronger. When such talismans and charms were burned, the demons were believed to be most satisfactorily roasted, tortured, and killed. For such important talismans, the gods were specially chosen from among Generals of the Celestial Armies.

Sentences in ordinary Chinese writing dedicated to gods and spirits to station themselves on certain spots to protect people feature in a good number of talismans. Among these, one finds commands like,

70, 72–3
74

81

64, 65

29

'Planet Jupiter take station here', 'Li Kuang shoot your arrows this way', or 'This is to order the Dark Lady of the Nine Heavens to stop murderous influences'.

The Taoist Vision

Taoist magic offered man an inner vision to help him communicate with the various spirits that inhabit the body. But since the body is a microcosm, all these interior spirits are also spirits of the exterior world. By the use of talismanic calligraphy, the Taoist is able to extract the cosmic emblems from within, and project them around himself as if forming a meditative mandala – his personal image of the universe, with himself at the centre. This image is sometimes reduced in talismanic magic to a mere circle representing the Whole, the Great Ultimate, the ultimate substance of Tao: emptiness. It is in perfect equilibrium, and nothing can harm it. It takes no initiative, to produce either happiness or disaster.

82

The spirit of philosophical Taoism remains the most important mystic ingredient in the occult use of talismans. This idea is best summed up in the words of an eighth-century Taoist source, the *Kuan-yin tzu*:

Being is Non-Being and Non-Being is Being; if you know this, you can control the spirits and demons. The Real is Empty and the Empty is Real; if you know this, you can see the stars even at dawn. . . . If you unite yourself with all things, you can go unharmed through water and fire. . . . Only those who have the Tao can perform these acts. Better still not to perform them, though able to perform them.

Indeed, talismanic magic was all this in essence. In practice, it provided the link between popular Taoism and Taoist philosophical mysticism. In the application of occult ideas, it harmonized sectarian views and teachings without necessarily discrediting any of them, or creating rivalries. Talismanic magic art encompassed the symbolism of the noise of the fire-crackers in popular spirit festivals as it did the silence of the Taoist hermit's meditation, recognizing both as ways of spiritual communication. Thus meditational inactivity existed happily alongside the vigorous dance movements within this frameless and endless system of multiperceptual symbolism, in which even time and space could be dissolved. For the true mastery of this magic art the understanding of Tao is needed: the understanding of the process of change, the harmonization of experiences, spiritual and human alike, which in the final analysis cannot be encompassed by a single act of will.

The Plates

Plates 1–17

Taoist magic diagrams are regarded as most potent talismans, with universal command over all spiritual forces. They invoke the harmonizing influence of yin-yang and Eternal Change, the Divine Order of Heaven, Earth, and Mankind, and the workings of the universe, through the principle of the Five Elements, symbolized by the Five Sacred Mountains, places of Taoist pilgrimage. In plates 1–10, meditative power is the dominant theme, and the shamanistic origin of the talismans related to the Five Sacred Mountains may be gathered from the hints of ritual masks. In plates 11–12, occult script forms accompany talismans related to Directions and Seasons. Plates 13–15 illustrate the magic power of the Divine Order resulting from the unity of Heaven and Earth, expressed in a variety of different ways – for instance, rolling clouds (Heaven) lend their shapes to rock-formation (Earth) – and used in a variety of talismanic magic (plates 16, 17).

1 The Blessed Union of *Yin* and *Yang*. The characters at the foot of the diagram, *ting-men*, mean 'Summit gate'. *Ting* also means the button or knob a Taoist wears on his cap. This *ting* symbolizes the *ch'i* (Vital Energy) which accumulates at the top of the head through Taoist self-cultivation. The chief Taoist technique for increasing Vital Energy, refined through the system of internal circulation, is the sexual practice of coitus reservatus. (*Tao-tsang* 550–3:3a)

2 The Pattern of Change, produced by the intercourse of the Vital Energy of Ling-pao with the Vital Energy of primordial darkness. The first of a set of three most powerful and universal Taoist magic diagrams, related to both Heaven and Earth (see also *3, 4*).

3 The Space Song of the Blue Sky (*pi-lo*). *Pi-lo* also means 'the sound of Jade falling from Heaven'. The second of a set of three most powerful and universal Taoist magic diagrams, specially related to Heaven (see also *2, 4*).

4 The Dark Earth of the Great Float (the floating island of the Taoist Immortals). The third of a set of three most powerful and universal Taoist magic diagrams, specially related to Earth (see also *2, 3*).

The set of three (*pls. 2–4*) is preserved in the present form in a Sung work attributed to Emperor Hui-tsung, 1101–26. (*Tao-tsang* 144–1:2a, 3a, 4a)

5 The marbled pattern of *ch'i* (Vital Energy) painted on the forehead in theatrical make-up designed by the modern Chinese artist Hao Shou-chen (1886–1961). This make-up recalls the shamanistic masks used in Taoist magic. Chinese theatrical masks carry on the same tradition.

6–10 Five is the most important number in Taoist magic. The five great mountain peaks of China are taken as the repositories of the spirits of the Five Directions (N, S, E, W and Centre), and as the source of the corresponding Five Elements (see p. 11).

These five diagrams are, according to the Chinese captions, the Talismans of the 'True Forms' (i.e. the authentic, pilgrim-protecting talismanic forms) of the Sacred Mountains of the East (T'ai-shan in Shantung); South (Heng-shan in Hunan); West (Hua-shan in Shensi); North (Heng-shan in Hopei); and Centre (Sung-shan in Honan). The primitive, shamanistic imagery is left unexplained in Chinese sources, though it seems to preserve some representational elements of local spirit-cult images. (*Tao-tsang* 849:11b, 12a, 12b, 13a, 13b)

11–12 Talismans of the 'True Forms' of the Sacred Mountains (see also *6–10*), combined with magic graphs for the corresponding directions and seasons. The Sacred Mountain of the North Talisman has graphs for North (above) and Winter (below). The Sacred Mountain of the East Talisman has graphs for East (above) and Spring (below). These talismans are attributed to the legendary Tung-fang So, the Chinese equivalent of Baron Münchhausen, who is supposed to have lived during the Han dynasty, 2nd century BC. (*Tao-tsang* 438:11b–12a, 8b–9a)

13 A cluster of sacred Taoist spirit fungus, modelled with rolling clouds which are the secret locations of spirits. Like the gnarled roots in *pl. 14*, its eroded shape harmonizes *yin* and *yang*, Heaven and Earth. Their harmony has supernatural power combined here with the efficacious medicinal power of the *ling-chih* fungus. (Porcelain, *kuan* type, Yung-cheng seal-mark, 1723–35)

14 Earth (*yin*) is represented by twisted root and branch shapes, and Heaven (*yang*) by the holes between them, resembling constellations. The side-views of this stand provide two different esoteric diagrams for locating spirits. (Carved wood stand, Sung dynasty style)

15 The diagram of the Mountain of the Blue City, also known as the Mountain of the Heavenly Kingdom, includes secret passages for man to reach the spirits who dwell up among the mountains. The mystic symbolism of the shapes harmonizes rock formations (*yang*) and cavities (*yin*). The cavities are also seen as referring to constellations, adding to the power of the unity of Heaven and Earth. Attributed to Tung-fang So, who was supposed to have lived during the Han dynasty, 2nd century BC. (*Tao-tsang* 438–14a)

16 South-orientated magic map of the Lanterns of the Nine Hells, used symbolically to guide souls out of Hell, and help them to escape various forms of torture. (*Tao-tsang* 217–14:5b)

17 'Scattering *ch'i* in Bird Patterns': a diagram used in Taoist weather ceremonies to disperse clouds. (From a 19th-century Taoist weather manual)

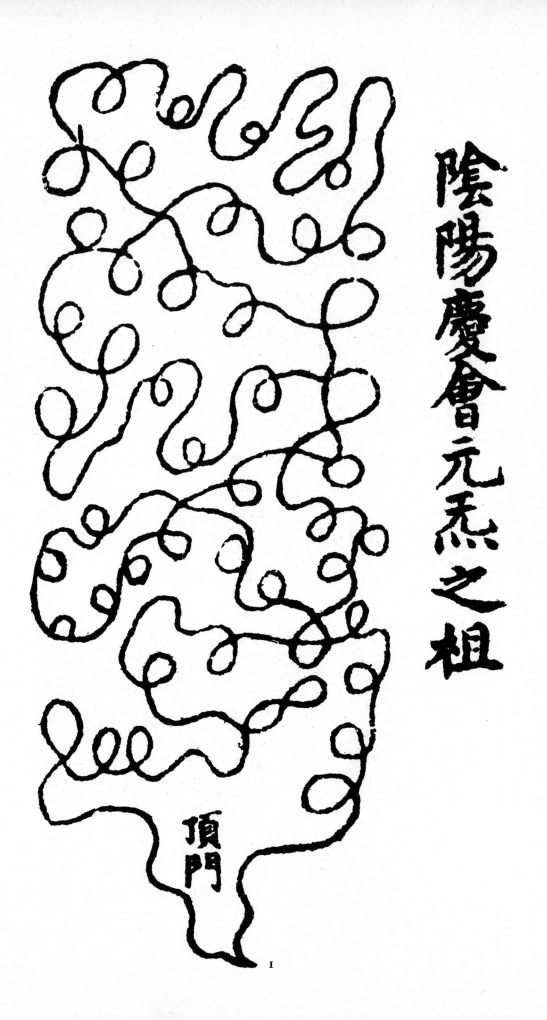

陰陽慶會元炁之祖

頂門

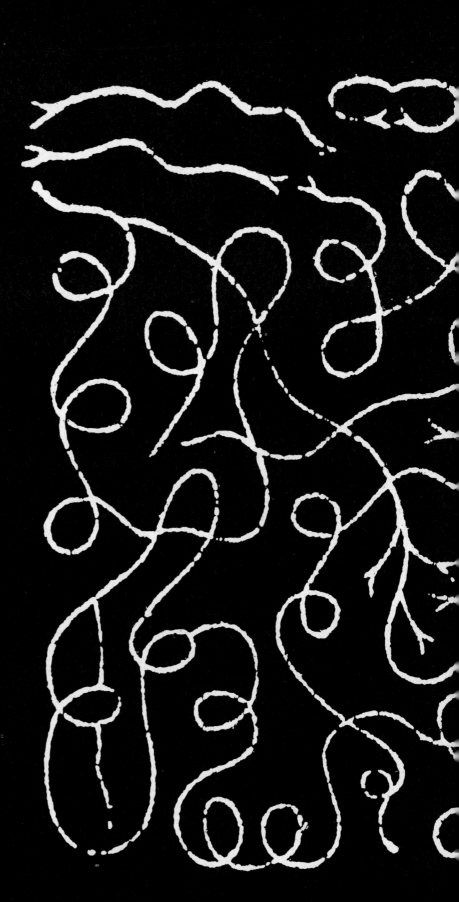

圖之化變

靈寶始青

歌之圖

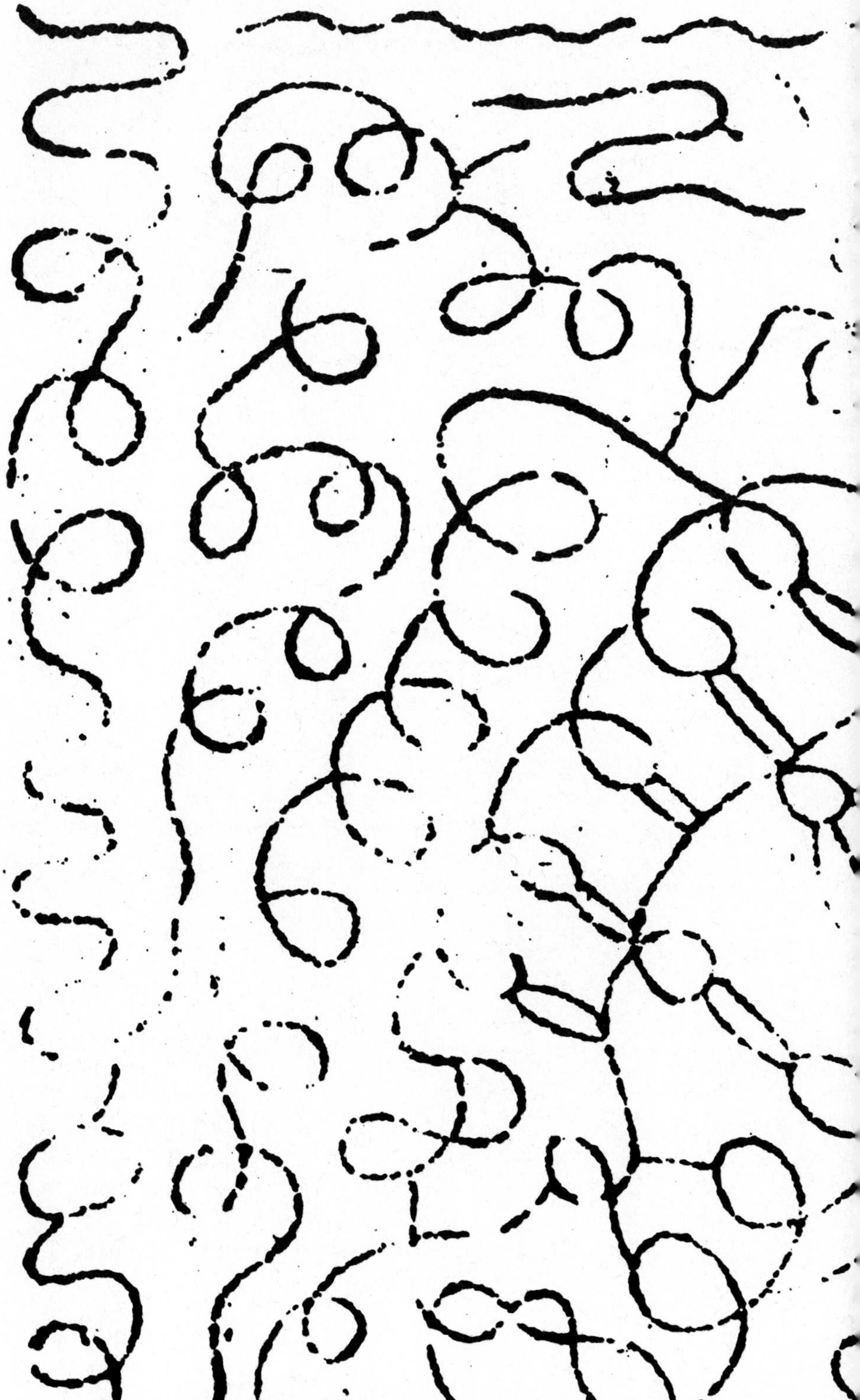

空落碧

大浮黎

5

東嶽真形符

6

7

西嶽真形符

西嶽

北嶽真形符

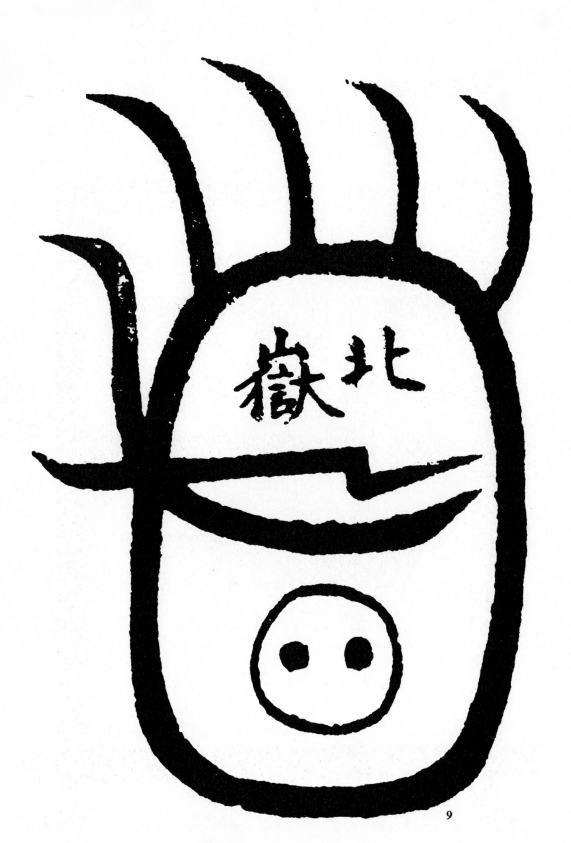

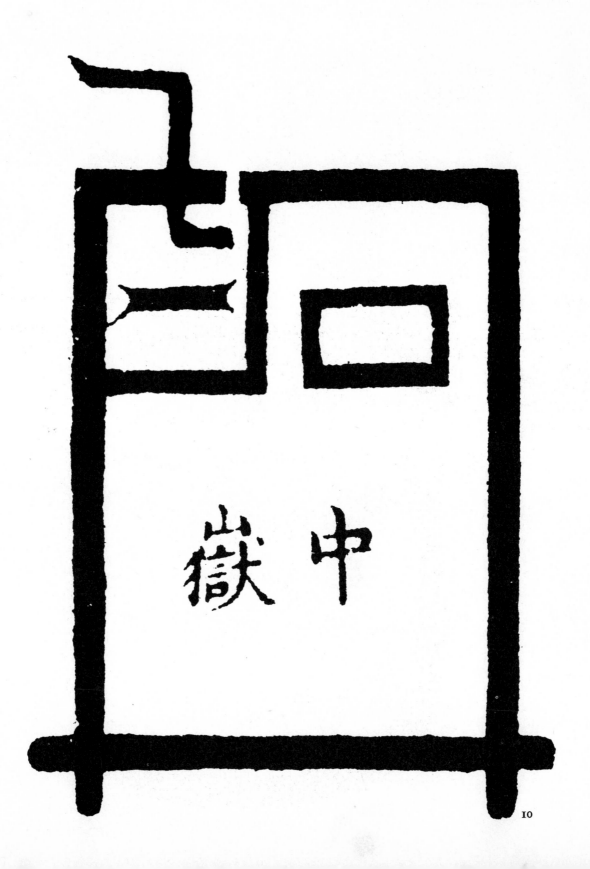

中嶽真形符

中嶽

北冬

北嶽常山真形圖

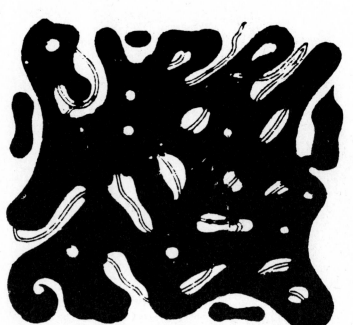

11

東春

東嶽泰山真形圖

12

13

14

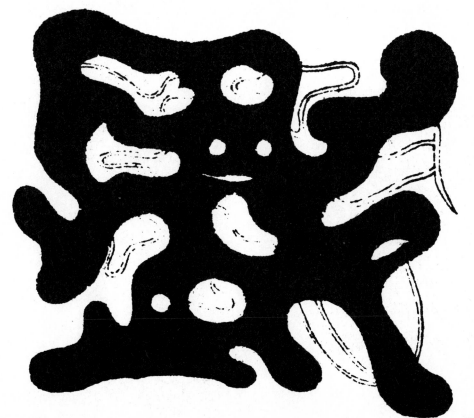

青城山一名天國山

15

沔氣島精

Plates 18–30

As testimony to human anxiety, Taoist magic is much concerned with immortality, or at any rate with the desire for a long and sexually active life. The life-giving talismans of Ling-pao, 'Spiritual Heavenly Worthy', Lord of Earth, represent some of the most powerful charms in this group, all of which are executed in a characteristically bold and heavy graphic style. These life-giving talismans seem to have been used in many different ways, including even in burial ceremonies (plate 19), but they all relate to a spiritual power which was closely connected with the ancient cult of the Earth Spirit. Birds (later more specifically cranes) represent longevity in occult tradition, hence their frequent appearance in talismans, often in shorthand form, for instance as bird-heads. These are the forerunners of the mystic Bird Script of talismans of later periods.

18 Talisman of the Armour of Earth. Eight *t'ien* (Heaven) characters surround a *kuei* character. *Kuei* spirits are the *yin* part of the soul after death, associated with demons or evil, or the souls of men who have not been properly returned to the earth in burial. (*Tao-tsang* 853:16b)

19 Bold Taoist talismanic calligraphy symbolizing Earth combined with 'constellation holes', i.e. Heaven. It was reputedly engraved on stone on the outer coffin of Duke T'eng of the Han period, *c.* 200 BC. (The earliest reference to this inscription is by a writer in the 6th century. Reproduced from the *Hui-t'ang che-chi*, 7b, late 14th century)

20, 21 Four magic formulae to ward off evil (*yin*) influences are combined in the design of this wooden stand, and also in the brushed composition which can be read from any of the four directions. It incorporates the characters for Heaven, Earth, Fire and Metal. (Stand, Ch'ing dynasty, 18th century; diagram, Sung date, *Tao-tsang* 543–38:18a)

22 Talisman to vitalize the tongue. Such diagrams in heavy calligraphy are an 'improved' version of the blood-stained impressions formerly made on the paper by the cut tongue of the medium. Attributed to Ling-pao. (In an early 12th-century work by Lin Ling-su, *Tao-tsang* 463–268:1b)

23 Talisman to vitalize the tongue. It is to be used under the sign of the third branch of the Twelve Earthly Branches, with corresponding symbolic animal Tiger, zodiacal sign Gemini, hours 3–5 a.m., and point of compass East-North-East. It represents the Vital Energy (*ch'i*) of the purple clouds of the Centre of Heaven. It is painted in cinnabar-red on a yellow ground. Attributed to Ling-pao. (In an early 12th-century work by Lin Ling-su, *Tao-tsang* 463; reproduced here from *Tao-tsang* 543–41:20a–b)

24 Talisman of the Bird Mountain of the Supreme Taoist, where Vital Energy gives life to the spirits. It is reputed to have the power to grant immortality. (Probably from the period of the Six Dynasties, *Tao-tsang* 431:5a)

25 Jade Talisman symbolizing ascending *yang*, with the Dragon of the East and the Fire Bird of the South. A talisman to prolong active life and increase sexual energy. (Period of the Sixth Dynasties)

26 Talisman in brushed technique, used to establish contact with spirits and/or to bring about Unity. Like the talisman in *pl. 23*, to be used under the sign of the third branch of the Twelve Earthly Branches. It represents the Vital Energy (*ch'i*) of the precious radiance of the Centre of Heaven. Painted in cinnabar-red on a yellow ground. Attributed to Ling-pao. (In an early 12th-century work by Lin Ling-su, *Tao-tsang* 463; reproduced here from *Tao-tsang* 543–41:17a–b)

27 Talisman to vitalize the kidneys (kidneys symbolizing the female sex organs). The two shapes suggest a pair of female dancers with *yin* receptacles (i.e. the female sex organs) emphasized. To be used under the sign of the first branch of the Twelve Earthly Branches, with corresponding symbolic animal Rat, zodiacal sign Aries, hours 11 p.m. to 1 a.m., and point of compass North. It represents the Vital Energy of the dark clouds of the North. Black on a white ground. Attributed to Ling-pao. (In an early 12th-century work by Lin Ling-su, *Tao-tsang* 463; reproduced here from *Tao-tsang* 543–41:18b)

28 Talisman to vitalize the eyes. To be used under the sign of the fourth branch (with corresponding symbolic animal Hare, zodiacal sign Cancer, hours 5–7 a.m., point of compass East), and tenth branch (i.e. Cock, Capricorn, 5–7 p.m., West) of the Twelve Earthly Branches, representing the Vital Energy of the radiance of the Sun and Moon. Blue on a white ground. Attributed to Ling-pao. (In an early 12th-century work by Lin Ling-su, *Tao-tsang* 463; reproduced here from *Tao-tsang* 543–41:19a)

29 Talisman to vitalize the brain. To be used under the sign of the Centre, i.e. Earth, representing the Vital Energy of the precious radiance of the Upper Heaven. Red on a white ground. Attributed to Ling-pao. (In an early 12th-century work by Lin Ling-su, *Tao-tsang* 463; reproduced here from *Tao-tsang* 543–41:22b)

30 Talisman to vitalize the blood. The design appears to represent a coiled snake. Attributed to Ling-pao. (In an early 12th-century work by Lin Ling-su, *Tao-tsang* 463–268:2b)

地甲符

此　　　　　滕　　　　　日

室　　　　　公　　　　　吁

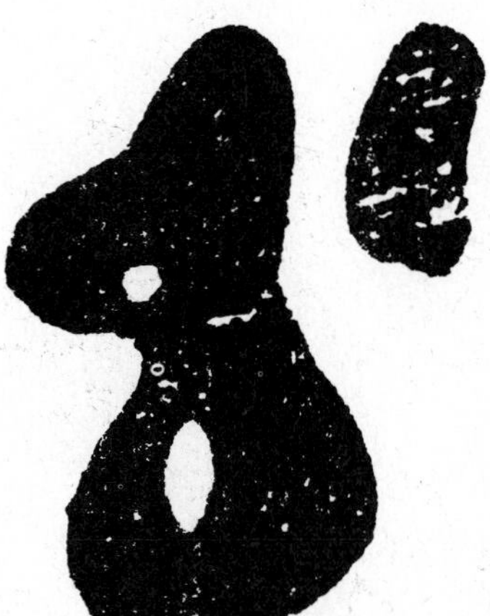

居　　　　　嗟

20

21

吾符

22

生舌符

寅文天中絳雲

之而黃地朱書

太上人烏之山岐雨鄲命天天不地不玩不浮雁畚師道畚鬼竹喟元虎衄迄

元萆干臨玩于所兆主山本禪盲玉乔澄河俥秦成走狗主辨仙也

24

25

生結符

窗丈天中瑶光

之燕黄地丹書

生腎符

子文北方黑雷
之炁白地思書

27

生目符

卯日大日月光
昼日月光
然白地青畫

28

生腦符

畫七中大上天寶光

之烈白地赤書

血特

30

Plates 31–41

The movement of air, and the rising smoke of incense and burnt paper talismans, represent ceaseless change and cosmic energy (ch'i) – the all-pervading force in Taoist magic. These highly abstract compositions have a characteristically thin and refined linearity. Their lines can be broken (yin) or continuous (yang), rounded (yin) or angular (yang), or a combination of both (plate 36). Although they are of widely different esoteric functions, ranging from charms for summoning spirits (plate 31) to medicinal talismans (plate 40), they are all related to Heaven, the yang partner of the yin Earth. This linear talismanic graphic style had a marked influence on the free calligraphic exercises of conventional Chinese art. The majority of them, however, were not originally painted with the brush. Most of them are derived from magic drawings by mediums on sand- or rice-tables.

31 Spirit-invoking esoteric diagrams formed by lines of blue and red. The diagram on the right invokes: 'the Immortals of the Great Paradise, the Supreme Heaven, the Five Sacred Mountains, the Four Great Rivers [Yangtze, Yellow River, Huai and Chi], the Twelve Sources of Rivers, and the Five Internal Organs [kidneys, heart, lungs, liver, spleen].' The diagram on the left invokes: 'the Super-Immortals of the Great Paradise and Supreme Heaven, the Feathered and Flying Divine Immortals and Fragrance-spreading Strong Men, each to represent the strength of 3,000 men.' (*Tao-tsang* 1367:15b)

32, 33 The eighth and twelfth of the Twelve Field-Marshal Talismans, by means of which Vital Energy (*ch'i*) stimulates the gall and heart respectively. The pattern suggests the rising smoke of incense. White on a blue ground, and white on red, respectively. (*Tao-tsang* 216–62:9b; 216–62:10b)

34 Talisman of the Charcoal-stove, based on the patterns of rising smoke. One of a set of eight diagrams to free souls from the Eight Tortures of the Earthly Prison (i.e. the charcoal-stove, the iron couch, the pile of knife-blades, the hollow bronze pillar with furnace inside, the boiling cauldron, the iron wheel, saw and ice). The text reads: 'By the will of this Ling-pao Talisman, liberate the dead on behalf of [so-and-so], get them out of the Earthly Prison of the Charcoal-stove, so they can ride on this

light and live according to the principles of human kind . . .' (*Tao-tsang* 216–51:15b)

35 Talisman to purify the mind, to be burned using an incantation of 37 characters which may be translated as follows: 'Spirit of the Divine Ruler of the Red Palace, Energy of burnt offerings, follow the light and fly to purify. Come to the cottage-wall of the Taoist so that weariness has no place in his mind. Under the peaceful morning sky the sweet dew sets quickly to form red jasper. Follow without delay the commands of the True Order.' (*Tao-tsang* 217–30:22b)

36 Old Master's Talisman to rid dwellings of evil spirits and cure epidemics, in combined round and square calligraphy. One of a set of seven, this charm is to be used only in the eastern quarters of the house. The others in the set are specified for the southern, western and northern quarters, and those to be placed on the bed, the stove and behind the house. (*Tao-tsang* 217–24: 16a)

37 Talisman to vitalize the lungs, in rounded (*yin*) calligraphy. To be used under the sign of the tenth branch of the Twelve Earthly Branches (corresponding to Cock, Capricorn, 5–7 p.m., West). It represents the Vital Energy (*ch'i*) of the yellow clouds of the Centre of Heaven. Painted in white on a black ground. Attributed to Ling-pao. (In an early 12th-cen-

tury work by Lin Ling-su, *Tao-tsang* 543–41:21b; also reproduced *Tao-tsang* 463)

38 Jade Talisman of Supreme Ruler One of the Great Cave, in rounded (*yin*) calligraphy. It embodies 'the turbid torrent of the whirlpool of the female essence', and 'offers a magic formula to ward off evil influences'. (*Tao-tsang* 7–2:21b)

39 Talisman of the Heavenly Cure, made in 1974 at the Chinese New Year. This type of mystic 'paper money' is known as 'white gold' in Singapore today. (Red ink and eight-trigram seal-impression on yellow. From a Chinese Taoist temple in Bukit Timah, Singapore)

40 Talisman of the Heavenly (*yang*) Cure for women (*yin*), with erect penis (*yang*) under a constellation. The penis carries a brushed character meaning 'induced to come'. The character also means 'by imperial order'. The curative diagram is based on the concept of illness (excess of *yin* influence) being cured by re-establishing the right balance between *yin* and *yang* through sexual intercourse. (*Tao-tsang* 217–16:6b)

41 Natural rock-formation in Hong Kong, a place of pilgrimage for Taoist women. All-night lantern festivals take place here, connected with the talismanic cult of the Heavenly Cure.

謁請大洞玉清上宮五嶽四瀆十二河源練

五藏仙人各十萬人

謁請大洞玉清上宮超仙羽步飛行神仙傳

香力士各三千人

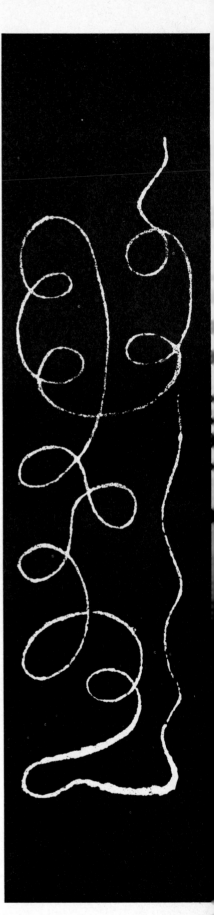

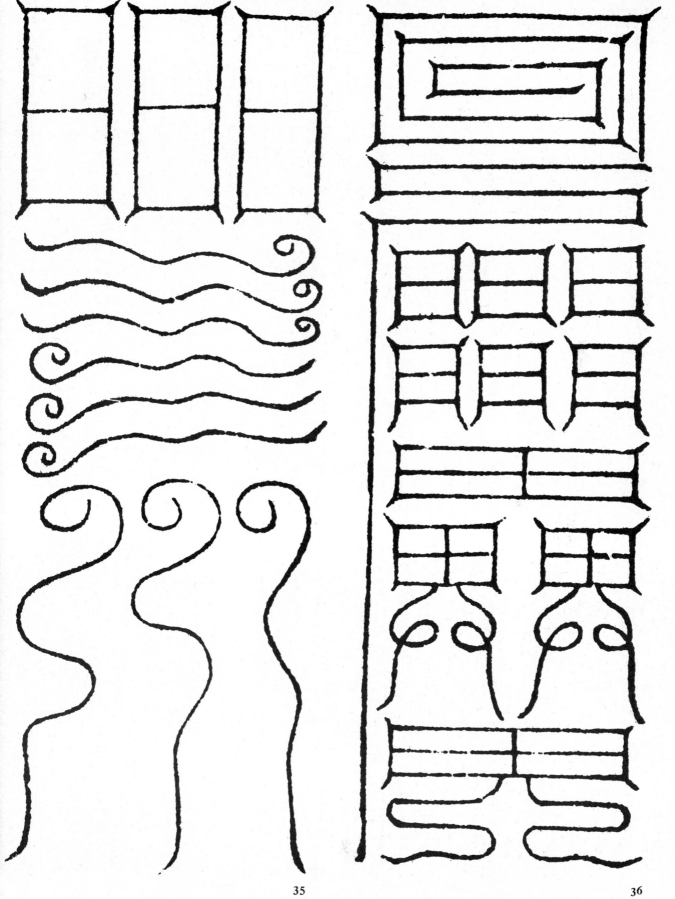

35   36

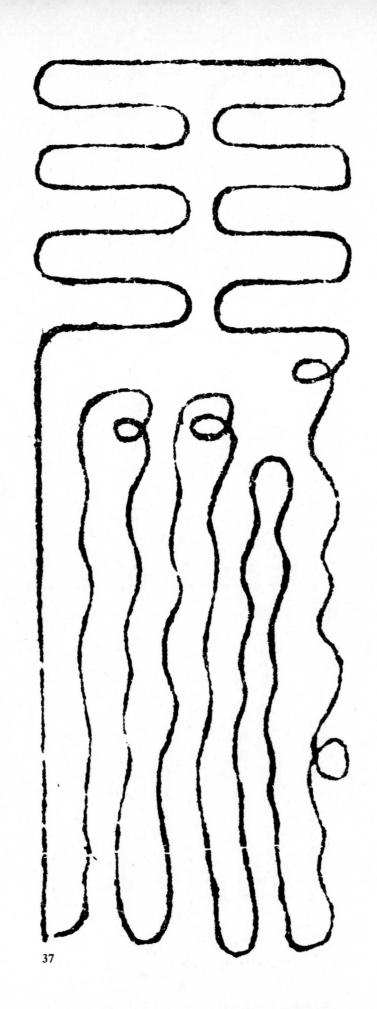

37

38

武吉大伯公

智者伯公

馬公

勅令

勅之係使合家平安世世

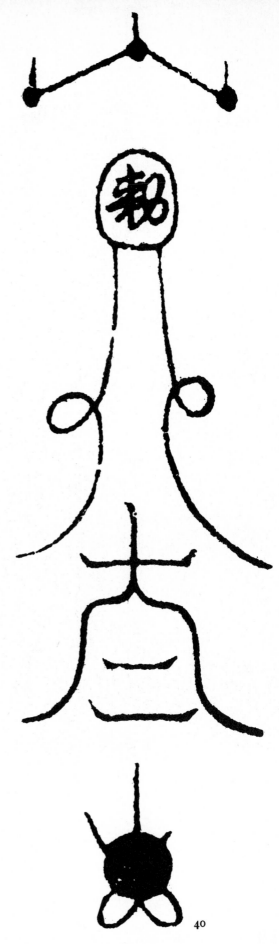

39

40

41

Plates 42–55

Cloud formations were associated with the movement of spirits, which were believed to dwell in mist, emerging suddenly to manifest themselves before human beings. A purple flash, or clouds of five colours, frequently marked such supernatural events. But these spiritual contacts too could be controlled by the magic power of calligraphy, and the various cloud-motifs employed in Taoist graphics serve this very purpose. Thus a variety of superbly linear and vapoury 'Cloud Script' forms derive their shapes and therefore their magic power from cloud formations. They are believed to have special powers to enable man to communicate with the spirit world, hence their extensive use in talismanic graphic art. Cloud formations, with or without constellations, also provide the model for the magic art of movement (plate 42), and even geomancy (plate 46). Sound was believed to penetrate this mysterious cloudy spirit world, so that talismans were often used in combination with spoken charms, incantations, and chants. The musical scores accompanying diagrams (plate 49) are written in a style resembling magic Cloud Script calligraphy.

42 Cloud Dance performed in mirror-image formation. The three pairs of female dancers represent the living, with the leg-movements of the *t'ai-chi ch'üan* exercises ('riding of the Heavenly Horse'), while their arm-movements symbolically reach out to invoke the spirits, in harmony with the Inner Alchemy. The Cloud Dance links microcosm and macrocosm, man with the spirit world. (Rubbing from a stone-engraving on an early T'ang tomb, excavated 1973–4)

43 'Flight of the Phoenix' around an imaginary ball of fire, i.e. the sun, an act of magic symbolically inviting the union of *yin* and *yang*, performed by acrobatic dancers of the Peking Opera. This movement expresses the same theme as the magic diagram shown on the facing page

44 Magic diagram of the interaction of the *yang* element of the fiery sun and flying *yin* rain-clouds. (Cinnabar-red and black ink. From a 19th-century Taoist weather-manual)

45 Diagram to prevent great rainfall and wind. The cinnabar-red sun collects black clouds in a fashion reminiscent of the geomancy pattern shown on the facing page. (From a 19th-century Taoist weather-manual)

46 Geomancy pattern known as 'The Flowing Spirits collect Water', indicating increased *yang* influence of the spirits which absorbs *yin* water and thus prevents rain. (From the geomancy manual of Chiang P'ing-chien, *Shui-ling ching* 1:35b, 1744 ed.)

47 Diagram for making rain, based on the seven-star constellation of the Great Dipper with a bird-headed cloud formation, symbolizing 'the bursting of clouds and rain', a metaphor for orgasm. In this esoteric context, sexual intercourse was believed to produce actual rainfall. Black ink. (From a 19th-century Taoist weather-manual)

48 Diagram of movement, based on the seven-star constellation of the Great Dipper, symbolizing, as the title states, 'the intercourse between Heaven (*yang*) and Earth (*yin*), in the footsteps method of the Great Yü (legendary emperor of the Hsia dynasty). These seven steps (the first and last footprints are not counted) also represent a ritual dance combined with sexual intercourse of man (*yang*) and woman (*yin*), at three different stages, indicated in the diagram by horizontal lines. (From an AD 1116 source, *Tao-tsang* 1210–8: 5a)

49 The waterfall – 'Mountain-peak Cloud Falls' – is made up of musical scores of hymns to the Immortals. These are recorded in the 'Sound of Jade' style of mystic calligraphy. (*Sleeping Dragon Mountain Scroll*, detail, attributed to Li Kung-lin, 1040–1106, of the Northern Sung dynasty)

50 The vertical linearity of the rock-face behind these musicians incorporates graphic elements of the 'Sound of Jade' style of calligraphy in musical scores of hymns to the Immortals. (*Te-hua* porcelain, early 17th century, Ming dynasty)

51 Taoist musical scores, relating to the mystic 'Sound of Jade'. (Collection of hymns to the Immortals, *Tao-tsang* 602–1: 9a)

52 Calligraphic exercise entitled 'Sound'. The character is executed by the contemporary Chinese artist Chiang Yee (who lives in New York) in the 'Sound of Jade' style of mystic script. (Shown at one-man exhibition Hong Kong 1972)

53 The Taoist Cloud Script (*yin*) employed as decoration on a brush-holder of phallic or rock (*yang*) shape. (T'ien-ch'i period, 1621–7, Ming dynasty)

54 An early 4th-century version of Cloud Script which seems still to retain talismanic graphic elements: the elongated strip-format of talismans dominates this style. Cloud Script was used to emphasize the unity of *yin* (clouds, mist etc.) and *yang* (Heaven). The standard forms of the Chinese characters are printed below. (*Tao-tsang* 78:33b–34a)

55 Text of *Primordial Tao*, an esoteric essay, written in Cloud Script characters with the standard forms of Chinese characters above. (Sung period, *Tao-tsang* 220–3: 12b–13a)

42

金充流火登天空白午时大雷雨

44

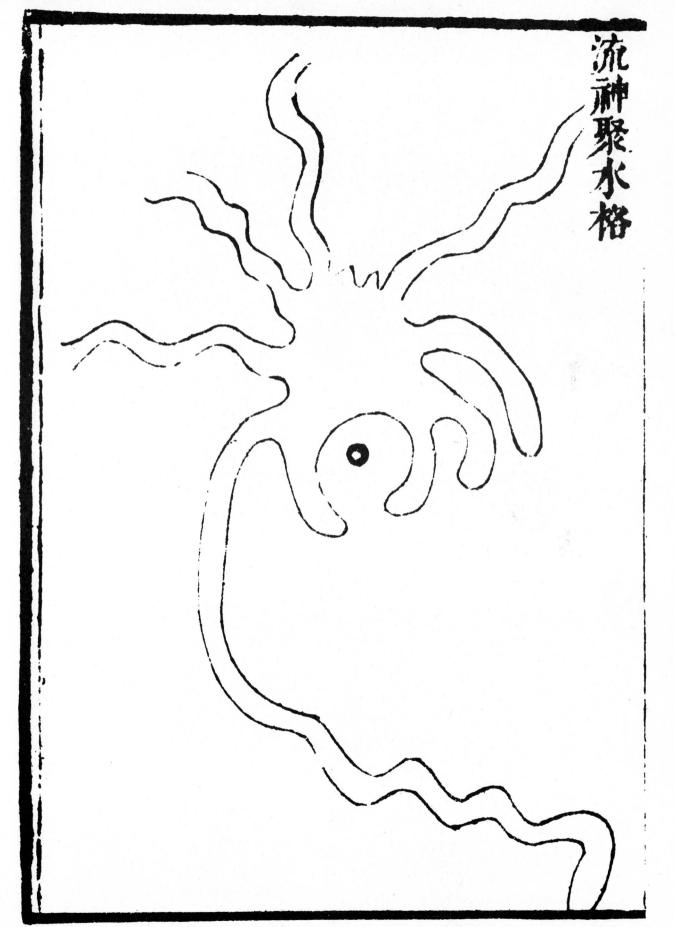

流神聚水格

46

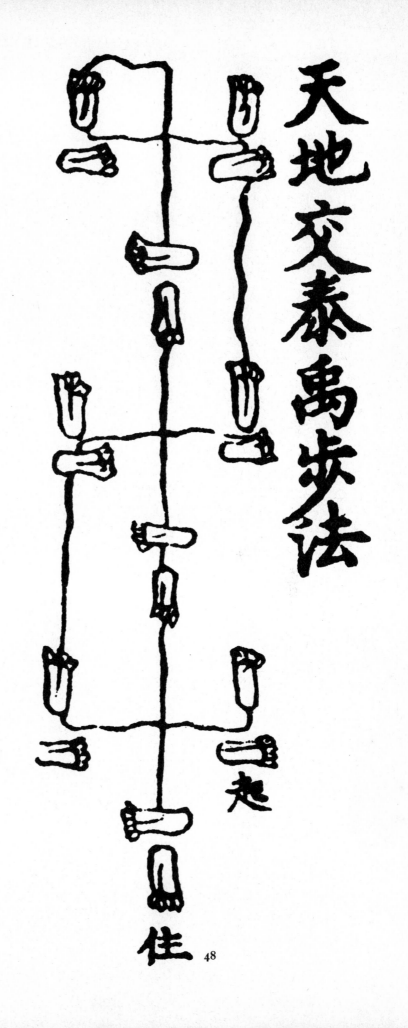

天地交泰禹步法

走

住

48

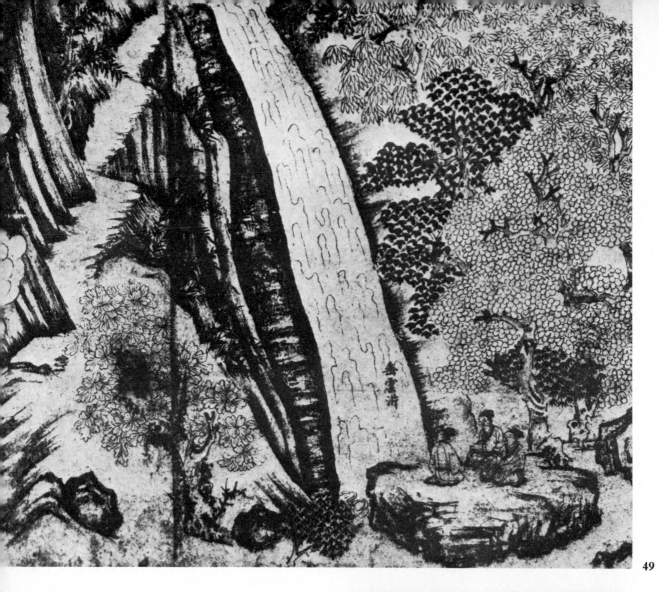

49

50

龍　萬　保　用　但　　厭　奉　不　靃　世

鱗　劫　智　當　在　年　戒　暫　世　善

風聲 雨聲 竹韻
松聲 芭蕉聲 少女聲
皆聲 山石皆可聽之聲也
滌邨唑并書 薛夔

52

53

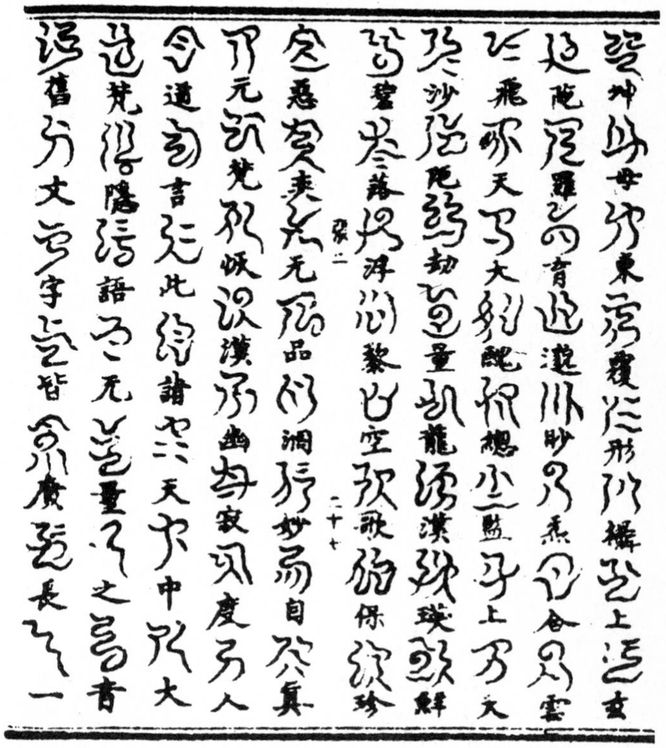

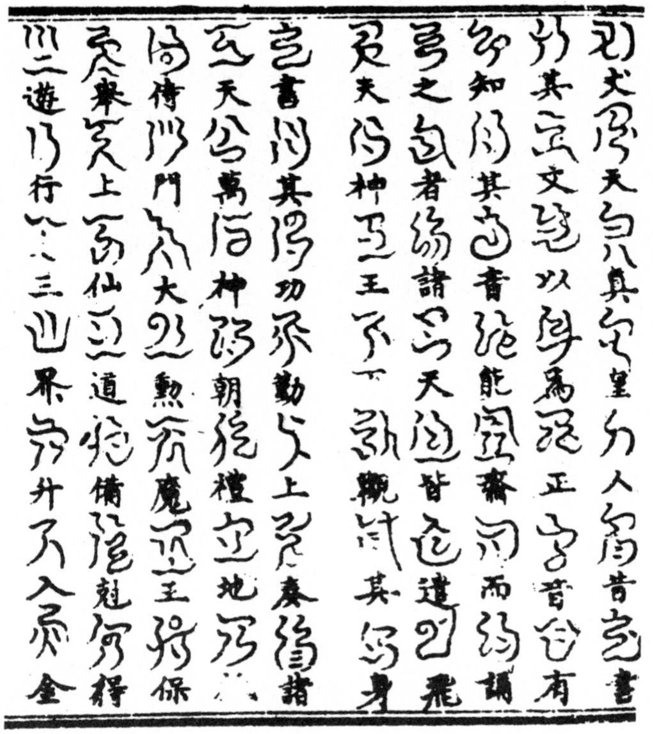

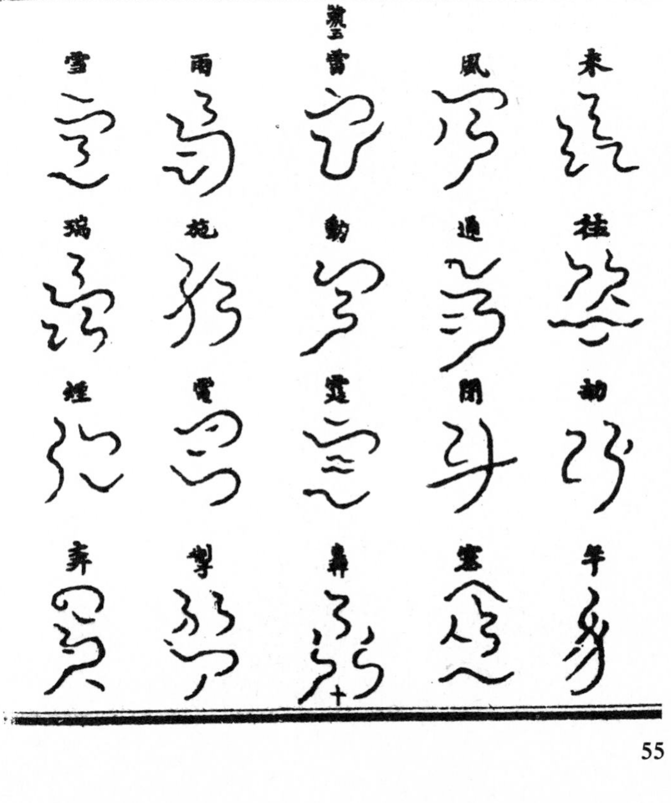

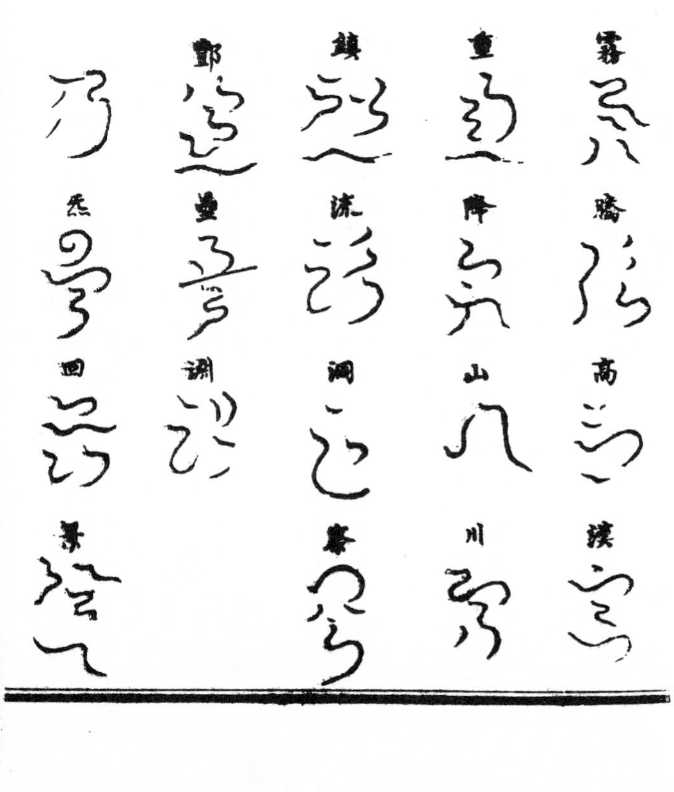

Plates 56–63

Invisible geomancy currents and their mysterious patterns form a special group among Taoist occult graphic diagrams. The purpose of these diagrams was to prevent danger and calamities, and to suggest locations which would enable one to avoid confrontation with spirits rather than to invoke them, so to that extent they differ from other talismans. The patterns included various 'scientific' observations of the invisible magnetic, wind, and underground-water currents of the Earth, relating them to the visible aspects of the location or landscape. As graphic diagrams they are powerful tools of sympathetic magic, enabling one to bring about many kinds of desirable changes. Their occult application is virtually unlimited. This is indicated by the titles of these geomancy patterns (as given in the captions below), many of which have sexual connotations.

Representational art makes full use of these forms (plate 57). These ideas were also employed with the utmost precision in the anatomical theory of yin *and* yang *diseases in traditional Chinese herbal medicine and acupuncture. They provide the concepts for the location of acupuncture meridians and spots to be stimulated 'to evoke' – as one would invoke spirits – either* yang *tonification or* yin *sedation, according to the prescribed intensity of stimulation of the affected areas and nerves. Names given to the body's hollows, and blood and breath conveyances, frequently suggest geomantic parallels.*

56 Geomancy patterns. The diagram above is entitled: 'A Beautiful Woman offering Flowers' (sexual reference is intended). The diagram below: 'The Pincers of a Centipede'. (From the geomancy manual of Chiang P'ing-chien, the *Shui-lung ching* 3:12a, 1744 ed.)

57 The 'One', the 'Great Ultimate', *t'ai-chi*, expressed in sexual terms as the magic union of *yin* and *yang*. The lovers are in the Taoist 'Hovering Butterflies' posture, the eleventh of the Thirty Heaven and Earth Postures. (Porcelain, mid-18th century, Ch'ing dynasty)

58 Geomancy pattern of the 'Great Ultimate' (*t'ai-chi*), represented as the union of interlocked *yin* and *yang*. (From the *Shui-lung ching* 3:11b, 1744 ed.)

59 Geomancy makes its appearance in a military handbook on explosives, dated 1662. Placed on a trigram *ch'ien* (*yang*), with legs apart, the female (*yin*) receives a phallic candle to produce an 'explosion', i.e. to produce orgasm. (From *Wu-lüeh chih* by Mao Yüan-i, 1662; recently reproduced in a Maoist article relating to guerilla warfare, by Lin Hsien-chou in *Wen-wu* 1973, entitled: *Invention of automatic devices: bombs, land mines and limpet mines in ancient China*)

60 The composition of this scene of lovers in a garden is reminiscent of the geomancy pattern known as 'A Lake peacefully Gathering Pebbles' – a Taoist metaphor for sexual intercourse. (Blue and white porcelain sleeve vase, Transitional period, *c.* 1640–60)

61 Geomancy pattern known as 'A Lake peacefully Gathering Pebbles'. (From the *Shui-lung ching* 1:53b)

62 Geomancy patterns known as 'A Boat Sailing with the Wind' (above), and 'Harbouring in a Cave with Bent Bow' (below). The title of the second has military as well as sexual connotations. (From the *Shui-lung ching* 3:16a, 1744 ed.)

63 Geomancy patterns known as 'An Immortal's Hands plucking the Lute (above), and 'The Left and Right Hands of an Immortal'. (From the *Shui-lung ching* 3:9b, 1744 ed.)

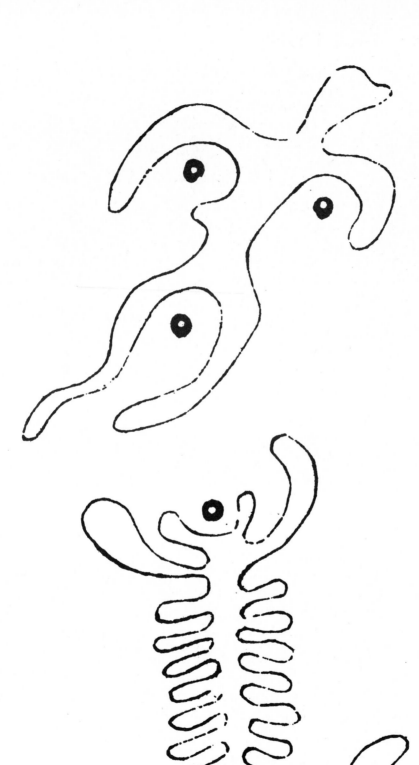

美女獻花格

蜈蚣鉗格

57

58

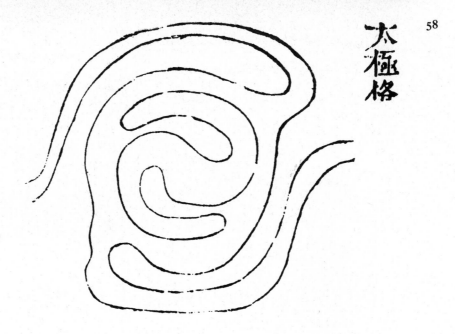

太極格

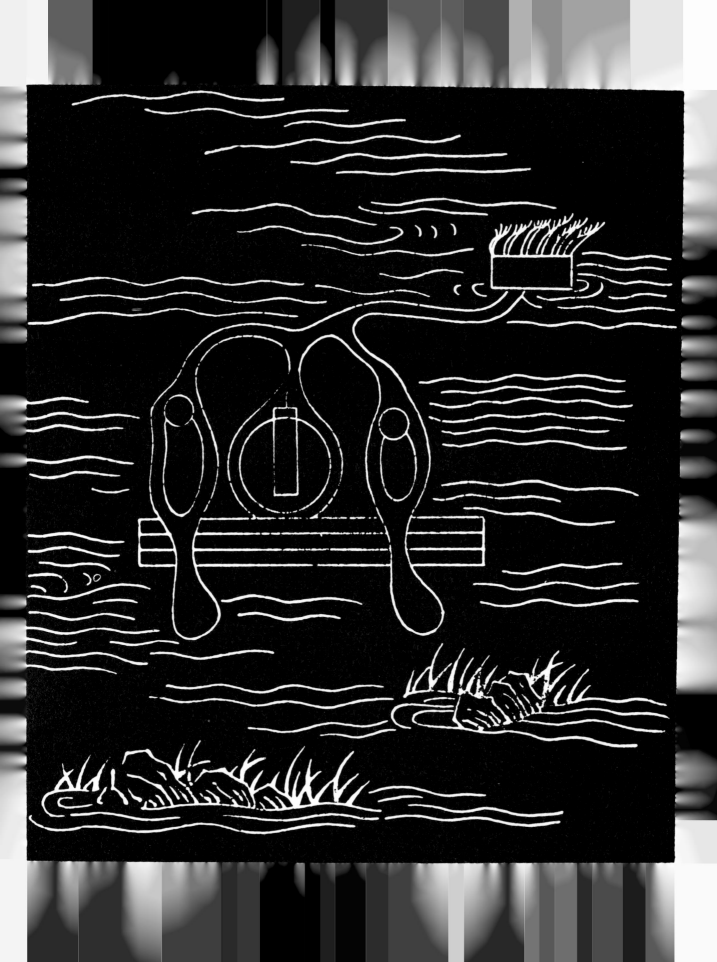

60

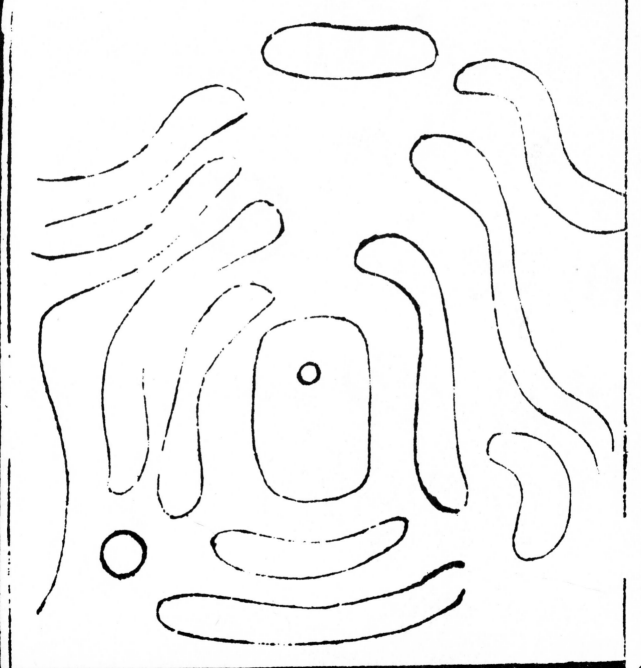

順風船格

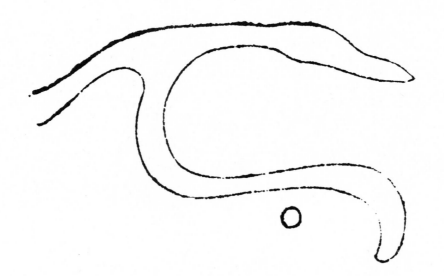

彎弓抱穴格

仙掌撫琴格

左右仙掌格

Plates 64–81

The magic ingredients of Taoist occult art were provided by their calligraphic components, some pictorial, others abstract, as well as by their general design. Extensive commentaries in the Tao-tsang *explain the components' significance, though mostly in characteristically laconic terms. For instance, in the Taoist canonical analysis of the magic components of the Jade Talisman (plate 66), the sequence of twenty diagrams reveals the order of the magic rites, and reflects the 'Journey of the Soul', guided by stars in heaven and by lanterns on earth. Charms containing characters for 'longevity', 'happiness', and 'good luck', executed in a variety of graphic styles (plates 73, 74) also form an important component group. They too are believed to work by virtue of sympathetic magic. Less common pictorial elements are human heads, legs and arms, which were supposed to confer exceptional power on composite talismans. These members are identified with the spirit figures of the popular Taoist pantheon. Some are executed with almost childish simplicity (plate 81), others skilfully incorporate magic characters of great complexity (plate 77).*

64, 65 Talismans of the fifteenth and twenty-fourth of the thirty-six Generals who act as Informers of Heaven, with both pictorial and abstract calligraphic components. Extensively used as 'paper money' for bribing spirits. (From an early 12th-century work, *Tao-tsang* 463–273:7b, 9b)

66 Analysis of the twenty components of the Jade Talisman (plate 67), from the Taoist Canon. According to the Chinese captions, these are (reading vertically and from the left): (1) the Eight Daybreaks which control the Wild Beasts; (2) the music of Emperor Shun which pacifies the subtle spirits; (3) the Nine Districts; (4) defects and melancholy; (5) Flying Creatures above the Spirits; (6) Close-netting and the Pure Region; (7) Fragrant and Beautiful; (8) the Empty Turn; (9) to pour a libation of Water; (10) the Yellow Flower[s]; (11) Period of Dark and Light; (12) the Master of the Spirits; (13) to open the Temple; (14) to prolong and yield; (15) the Cinnabar Hall; (16) the Four Directions; (17) the Six Rules; (18) the Thirteen Doors; (19) the Receiving of the Majestic Four Vital Spirits (*ch'i*); and (20) to pass by those who guard the Four Doors. This sequence seems to indicate the stages of an unknown ritual, while the magic ingredients of each diagram reveal multiperceptual contacts with the Yellow Spirit. (*Tao-tsang* 216–69:19b–20a)

67 The Jade Talisman, addressed to the Yellow Spirit, the powerful spirit of Earth and Centre. The third of a set of five (one for each of the Five Elements). (*Tao-tsang* 216:20a-b; based on the form attributed to Emperor Hui-tsung, 1101–26, of the Northern Sung dynasty: *Tao-tsang* 144–3: 13b–14a)

68 Script is used as magic on many objects. Here the stem of a plant is twisted into the auspicious character *shou* – 'longevity'.

(Blue and white porcelain bowl, Wan-li period, 1573–1619, Ming dynasty)

69 Sole surviving example of a secret Taoist script known as the 'Brilliant Jade Character' script. It gives a version of the first 48 (of 64) hexagrams of the I-ching. The script was used in talismans to refer to cycles of change, based on the trigrams of the I-ching. The style suggests the influence of embroidery. (In a work of AD 1115, *Tao-tsang* 463–262:30a)

70 *Shou* – 'long life' – at the centre of a dragon-and-cloud design representing the union of Heaven and Earth. The talismanic power of the *shou* character was believed to be so powerful that an object inscribed with it would certainly prolong the owner's life. Such objects were popular as birthday presents. (Carved red and black lacquer box-lid, Chia-ching period, 1522–66)

71 Belief in the magic power of calligraphy continues today in China. Chairman Mao's portrait is flanked in procession by double *hsi* ('happiness') characters, traditional Taoist talismans. The colour-scheme, red and green, is also Taoist, symbolizing the perfect harmony of Heaven and Earth. (Hopei Province, 1968)

72 Free brushed, 'grass' calligraphic form of the character *shou* – 'long life' – executed in the manner of a Taoist magic diagram. Signed by the 85-year-old Yeh Chih with the seal of the artist. (Rubbing dated 1st day of the 1st moon of 1863. Ch'ing dynasty)

73 The One Hundred Talismanic Forms of the character *shou* – 'long life'. (After De Groot)

74 The One Hundred Talismanic Forms of the character *fu* – 'happiness'. (After De Groot)

75 Talisman to repel demons, representing the devil-catching Chung Kuei. (19th-century stone rubbing)

76 Talismanic picture of the Taoist God of Literature, K'uei-hsing, made from two brushed characters forming his name. He stands on a third character, ao, the name of a giant turtle said to support the Earth. (Undated stone-rubbing; painted Ma Te-chao)

77 The seven characters of this calligraphic picture read: 'Tao penetrates Heaven and Earth and has qualities beyond Form'. They also depict the Star-god of Longevity. The rubbing is of an engraving said to be based on the Ho-t'u and Lo-shu diagrams (see p. 10). (Undated composition by Yüan Shen, painted by Tung Ts'e-san and engraved by Liu Kao-kuei)

78 Lanterns arranged as the characters *ch'ih yen sheng*, meaning 'to prolong life by imperial order'. A life-preserving talisman based on festive lantern-displays. *Ch'ih* ('by imperial order') has 49 lanterns, *yen* ('to prolong') 36, and *sheng* ('life') 24. As sources of light (*yang*), lanterns were supposed to help prolong active life. (From a 13th-century work, *Tao-tsang* 1210–9:15a)

79 Talisman for seeking employment. (From a Taoist work of unknown date, *Tao-tsang* 668–3:28a)

80 Talisman of the Armour of Man. The figure is reinforced with constellation dots. (Third of a set of three, probably Sung or Yüan in date, c. 1300, *Tao-tsang* 853:16b)

81 Talisman of the Heavenly Messenger, with coiled body representing the Twenty-eight Constellations to aid brightness (*yang*) and protect the body, and legs to walk in coils on Earth (*yin*) to seize and destroy evil spirits, who can only move in a straight line. (*Tao-tsang* 217–21:7a)

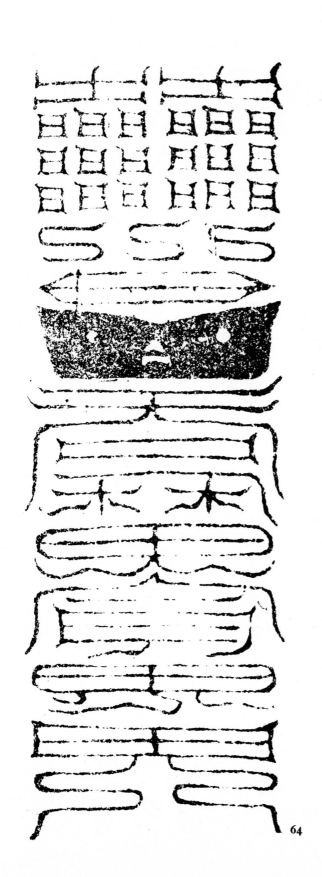

64

65

第三篇玉符

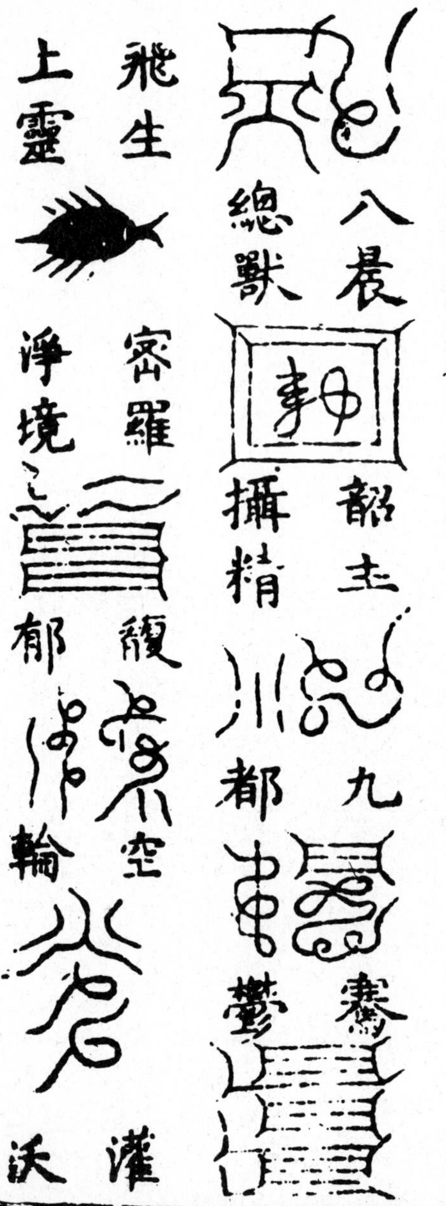

八晨　韶主　九

飛生　總獸　攝精　都　蕃

上靈　密羅　馥空　灌

出五　淨境　郁　輪　沃

十六

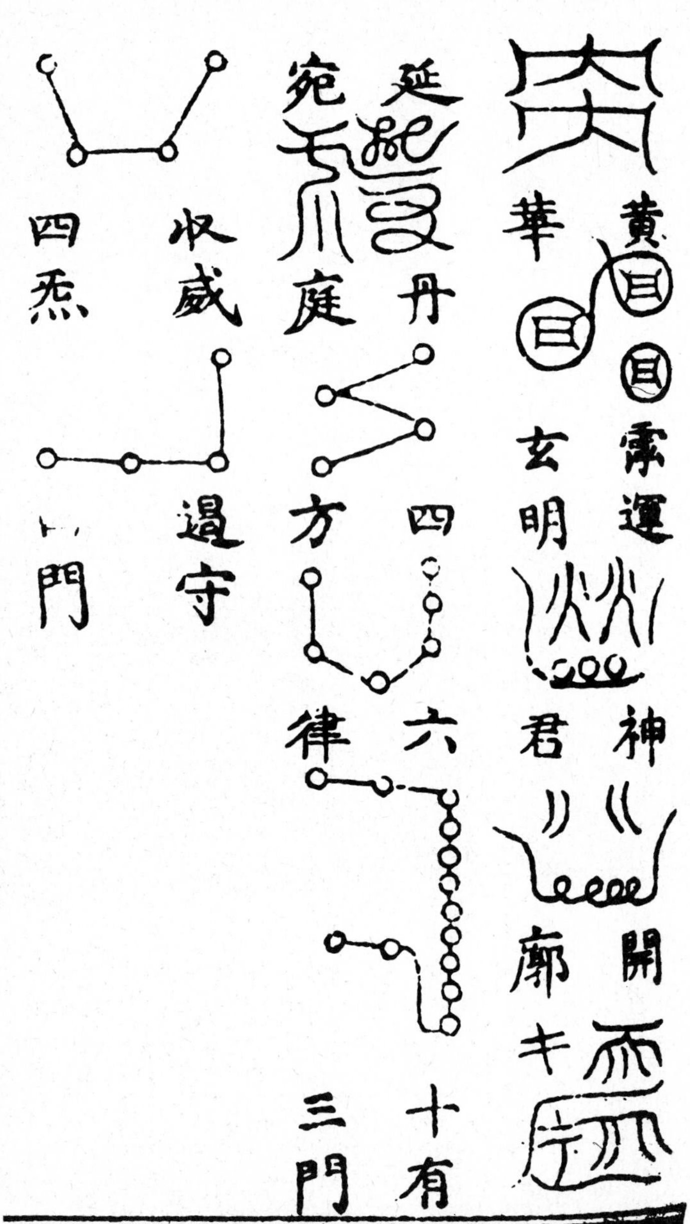

黃目　霄運　神　開

華目　玄明　君　廓　卞

延丹　四　六　十有

宛庭　方　律　三門

收威　過守　四門

二十六

二十四

70

71

同治癸亥正月元旦

八十五叟受葉志詵

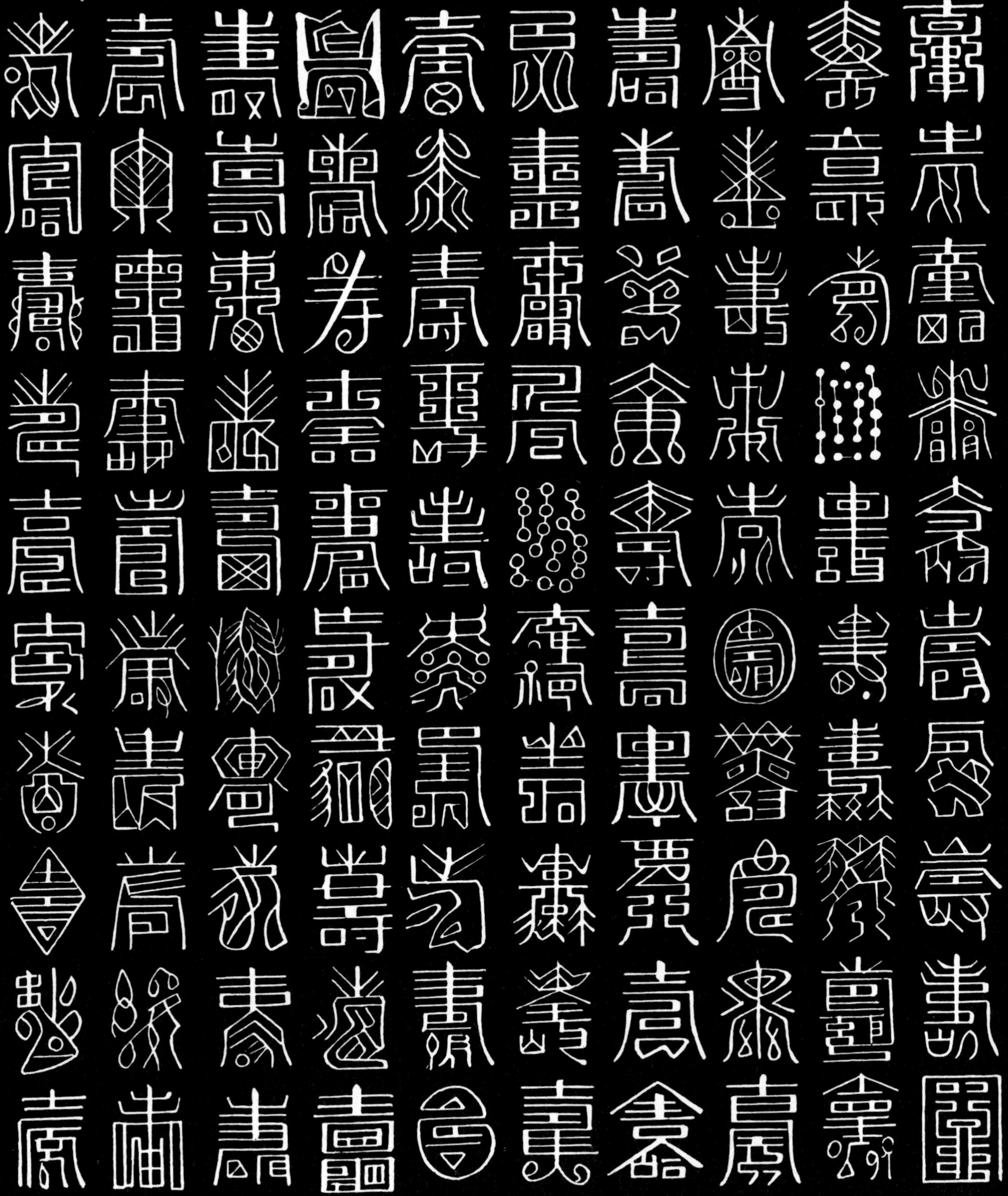

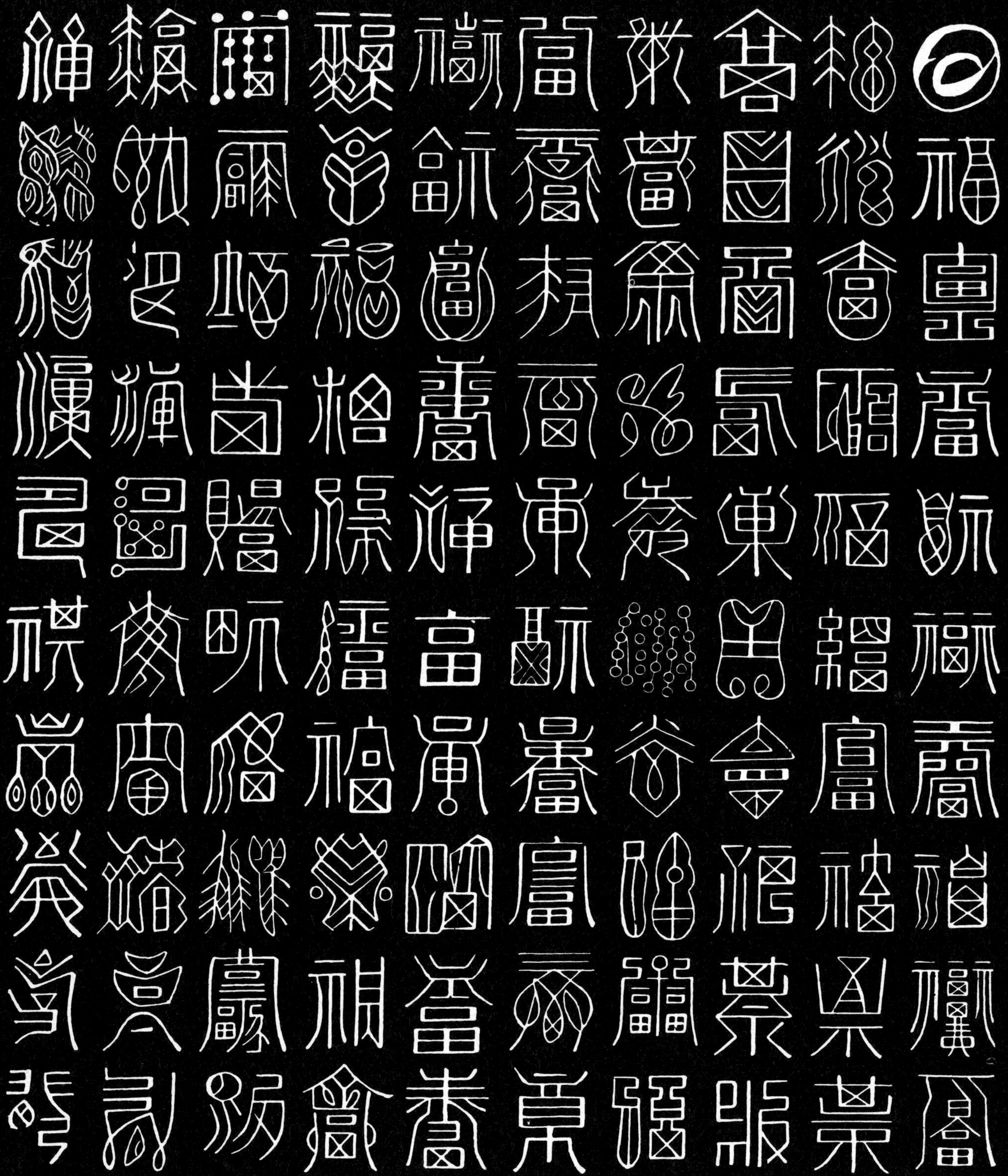

75

76

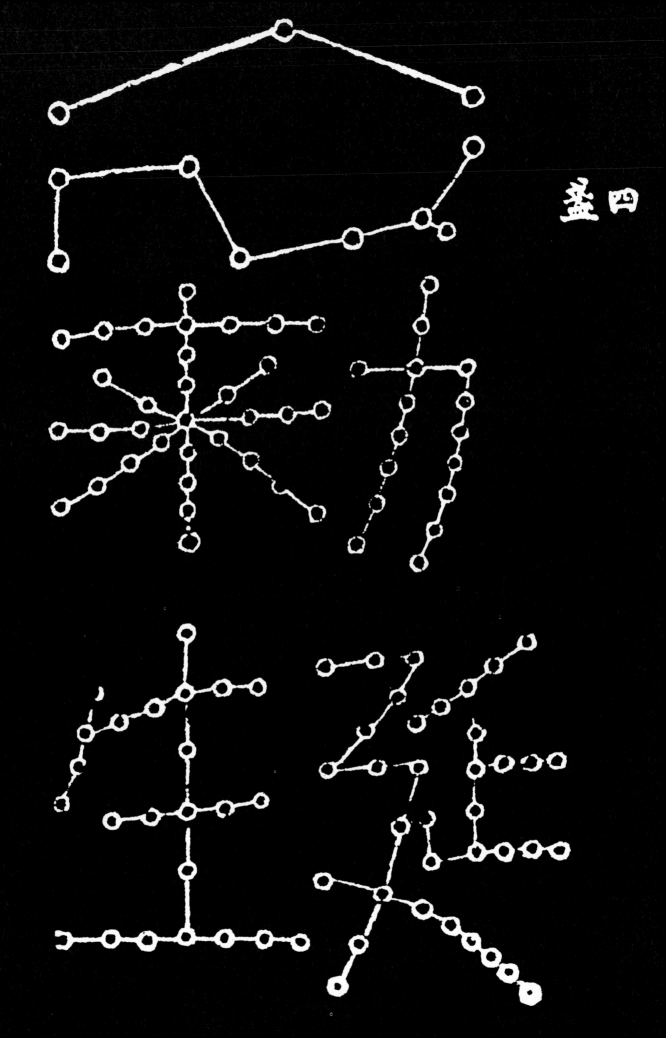

四盏

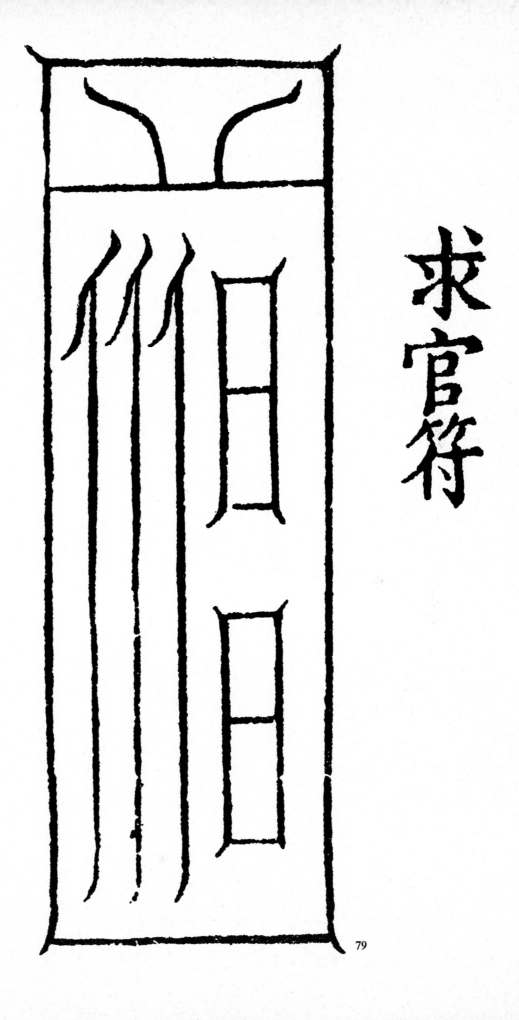

求官符

人甲符

天地人神
立设之精

行遍天下
收捉鬼神

二十八宿
助明护身

上天下地无所不经急
急收押入鬼心神君

诸将符

In Taoist magic art the circle combines simplicity with perfection, emptiness with fullness; it harmonized the visible with the invisible, the linear with cyclic manifestations of Change and Movement. Here it represents both the mystic and philosophical power of talismans (plate 83) and 'the One', the Great Ultimate (t'ai-chi) (plate 82).

82   Diagram of the Great Ultimate (*t'ai-chi*). (Yüan period, *Tao-tsang* 159–1:3b)

83   The 'Diagram of the Talisman' (*fu*). (11th c., Sung period. *Tao-tsang* 1210–5:5b)

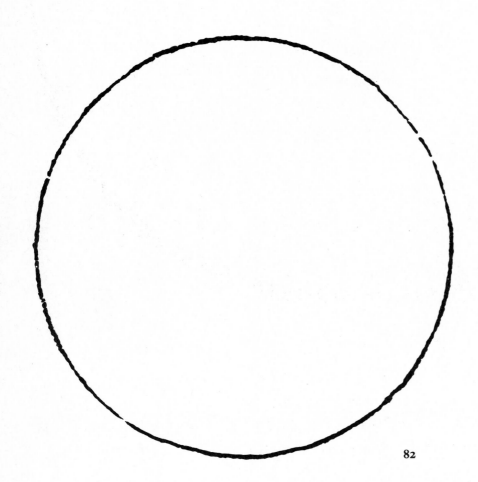

82

83

The Figures

三第

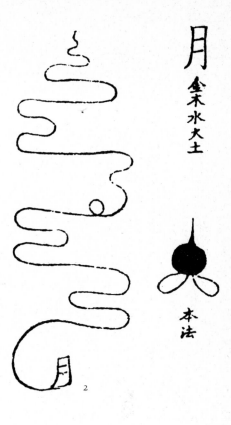

月
金木水火土
本法

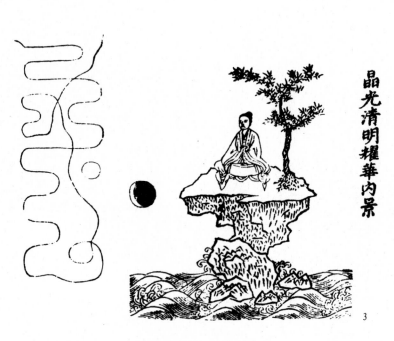

晶光清明耀華內景

Meditational diagrams and talismans

1 (Facing page) One of the Eight Pure Ones shown as a Taoist priest at an altar holding a phallic (*yang*) audience tablet in both hands, in a floating boat-shaped craft of rolling clouds. (*Tao-tsang* 426–3b)

2 The True Jade Talisman of the Ornamental Turn of the Moon. According to the caption the Moon represents the Five Elements. (*Tao-tsang* 217–18:5a)

3 The Beautiful Inner View of Brightness, Clearness and Splendour, depicting a meditating Taoist hermit on the right and a magic diagram on the left. The incantation to accompany the diagram may be translated as follows: 'The view spreads over Heaven [*yang*] and Lake [*yin*], Metal [West] and Water [North], in a semi-circle. To light the dark night, I and the Dark Pearl [the Moon in its last quarter] drink and drift [together]. The bright, thick liquid [of wine, *yin*] and its fragrance penetrate my spiritual body. After repeated true unions [with *yin*], I shall ride over the land and soar to the skies.' (*Tao-tsang* 218–1:12b–13a)

4 Nature-worship séance in an open pavilion, with a band of musicians left, potted dwarf-tree and miniature rock-formation centre, and sacrificial food and wine offered by Taoist priests right. (From a Sung dynasty work, *Tao-tsang* 437–2:15b–16a)

5

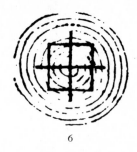

6

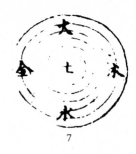

7

8

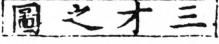

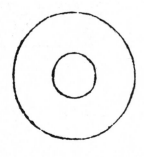

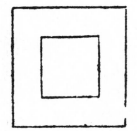

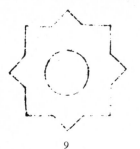

9

10

5 Magic diagram of the combination of the Five Element and Heaven and Earth diagrams. (*Tao-tsang* 217–24:24b)

6 Magic diagram of the round Heaven and square Earth. (*Tao-tsang* 217–24:24b)

7 South-oriented diagram of the Five Elements: Fire (and South) top, Earth centre, Water below; Metal left and Wood right. (*Tao-tsang* 217–24:25a)

8 Black Talisman in the shape appropriate to the Element Water with Cloud Script calligraphy. (*Tao-tsang* 853–17b)

9 Talismanic forms of *pi* discs appropriate to (top to bottom) Mountain (and Heaven) in blue; Earth in yellow; Water in black. (*Tao-tsang* 543–28:6a)

10 Diagram of the Three Sub-divisions of the Universe: Heaven, Mankind and Earth. (From the *I-hsiang t'u-shou wai-p'ien* by Chang-li of the Yüan period, *Tao-tsang* 159–1:4a)

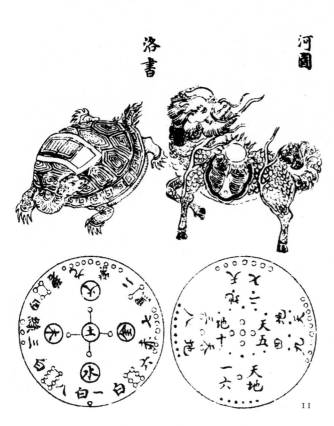

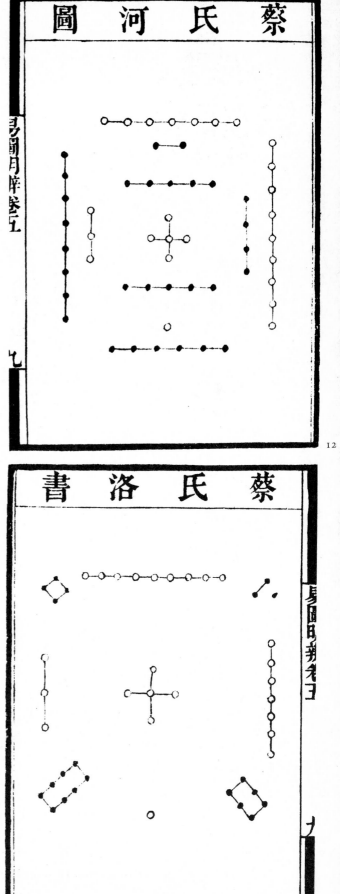

11 Diagrams of the legendary Taoist Ho-t'u associated with the Dragon-horse (right), and the Lo-shu associated with the Tortoise (left), showing magic arrangements of odd and even numbers within a circle. (From the *Ch'i-men* 5a, late 17th century)

12, 13 Diagrams of the legendary Taoist Ho-t'u (top) and Lo-shu, magic charts of odd and even numbers in rectangular arrangements according to the interpretation of Ts'ai Yüan-ting of the Sung period. (From a 1706 work by Hu Wei, the *I-t'u ming-pien* 5:9b, 9a)

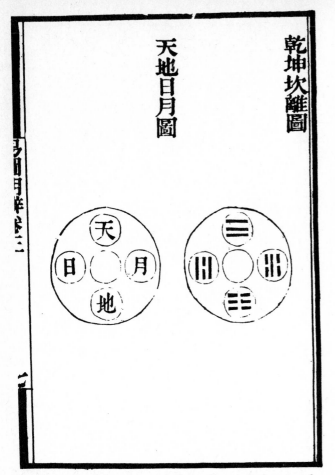

乾坤坎離圖

天地日月圖

文王八卦方位

14 Two magic diagrams symbolizing the universal power of Change. On the left: Heaven (top), Earth (below), Sun (left), and Moon (right). On the right: trigrams *ch'ien*, *k'un*, *li*, and *k'an*. (From a 1706 work by Hu Wei, the *I-t'u ming-pien* 3:7a)

15 The Eight Trigrams of King Wen, with South and trigram *li* (representing Sun) at top, North with trigram *k'an* (representing Moon) at bottom. (From a 1706 work by Hu Wei, the *I-t'u ming-pien* 8:6b)

天皇至道太清玉冊

血湖地獄燈圖　九宮八卦土燈圖

火德燈圖　九天玉樞燈圖

卷第五二十八

 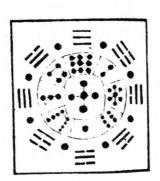 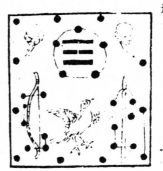 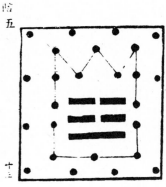

16 Magic diagrams of lanterns to guide spirits, composed of constellations and trigrams. From left to right: (i) the Jade Pivot of the Nine Heavens, (ii) the Power of Fire, (iii) the Eight Trigrams of the Nine Palaces, (iv) the Hell of the Blood Lake ('with red pebbles spread over the bridge'). (*Tao-tsang* 1460–5:28b–29a)

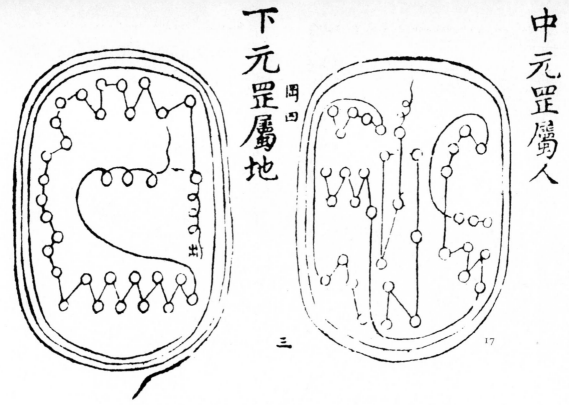

17　Two talismans to secure the orderly influence of the Five Elements, with magic constellations relating to mankind (on the right) and Earth (on the left). Two of a set of three relating to Heaven, Mankind, and Earth. (Early 12th century, *Tao-tsang* 217–19:3b)

18　Mystic diagram showing the combined Tread-pattern of Terrestrial Regulations and the Flight-pattern of Celestial Rules, to emphasize the magic union of Earth (*yin*) and Heaven (*yang*). In sets of foot-prints, symbolic of a ritual dance, Earth is represented by a mystic spiral of three complete turns, Heaven, by the constellation of the Great Bear, which is also repeated in the centre of the terrestrial spiral. A *yin-yang* regulator diagram of universal magic power. (Late 13th century, *Tao-tsang* 1210–8:3b)

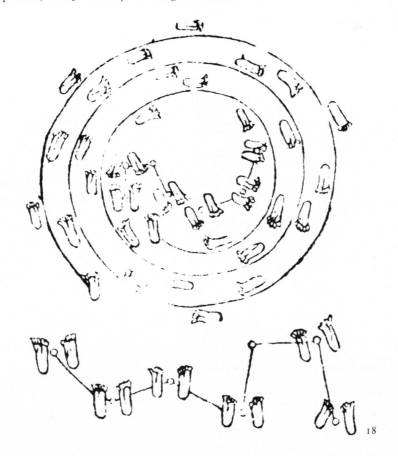

19

Charms for summoning spirits

19 Exorcist charm of the Supreme Heavenly Ruler of the South Pole, with special power to create law and order among evil spirits. (From an undated Taoist work on exorcism, *Tao-tsang* 1152–40:22b)

20 Talisman to protect the body in mountainous regions. The character *shan* – 'mountain' – forms part of the composition. This talisman is to induce the help of the Supreme Heavenly Ruler of the North Pole against baleful influence. (*Tao-tsang* 1152–38:2b)

21 Talisman for the Brief Spiritual Encounter Altar, to establish contact with the Spirits of Earth and Wind with the aid of the Spirits of the Five Emperors. To be burnt in front of the altar with an incantation of eight words. (*Tao-tsang* 1152–39:25a)

22 Exorcist charm of the Heavenly Messenger, who enforces law and order among the spirits and terminates the baleful influences of evil spirits. (*Tao-tsang* 1152–36:7b)

20

21

22

祈晴

23

24

23 Exorcist charm of the Five-Thunder Messenger who has special power to regulate rain and sunshine. (*Tao-tsang* 1152–40:14b)

24 Exorcist charm of a Heavenly Messenger riding a Dragon, to be used against the evil influences of Darkness (*yin*), with a 38-word incantation. (Early 12th century, *Tao-tsang* 217–25:4a)

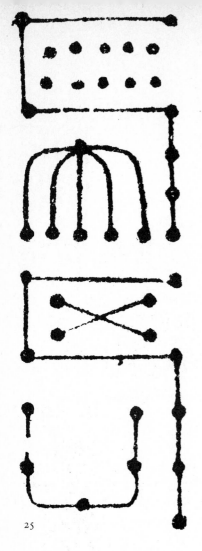

26

Preventive talismans

25 These two combined talismans bring good fortune if they are drawn on the wall when flies or bees fly into your house. The diagram is based on constellation dots. (*Tao-tsang* 668–2:11b, a section concerned with talismans for creating supernatural events)

26 A pair of magic taboo characters (in mirror image) incorporating the 'tiger' root, and thus the mysterious spirit of the tiger. They are to be used jointly to call home the soul of one who has died away from home. (*Tao-tsang* 217–17:10b)

25

27 Talismans to nullify the effects of cursing. Two of a set of five, one for each of the Five Directions. The talismans combine popular images of the Directional Supreme Rulers with magic diagrams that form their bodies. The White Supreme Ruler of the West is on the right and the Black Supreme Ruler of the North on the left. (*Tao-tsang* 217–10:6a)

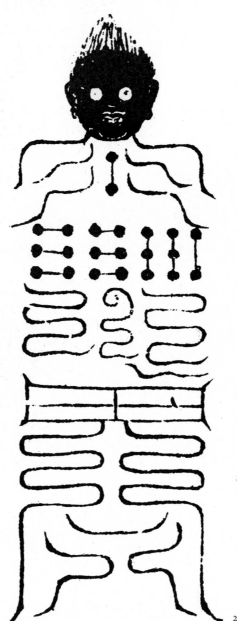

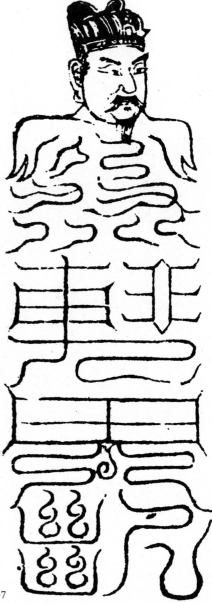

27

散雲符

28

止雨符

29

28 Talisman to scatter clouds. (From an undated Taoist work on exorcism, *Tao-tsang* 1152–41 : 30a)

29 Talisman to stop rain. (*Tao-tsang* 1152–41 : 30b)

30 A set of five magic diagrams: (i) to stop rain, (ii) to raise wind, (iii) to raise thunder (to strike those who are guilty of secret evils), (iv) to raise hail (to punish the evil), (v) to stop fog. (From the '*Secret methods of eminent spirits of purity and mystery*', *Ch'ing-wei shen-lieh pi-fa, Tao-tsang* 219–1 : 19b, a work of unknown authorship and date)

30

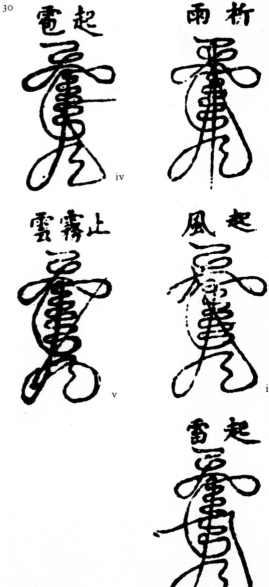

五字祕

電

風

雲

雷

31

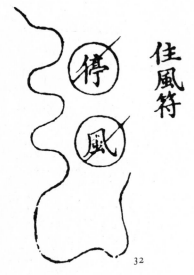

住風符

得

風

32

33 Talisman of the Jade Lady to repel *yang* influences. The talisman depicts the back (i.e. shadowed side) of a standing woman, thus doubly emphasizing the presence of *yin* essence in the composition. (Brushed calligraphic technique, *Tao-tsang* 217–21 : 5b)

31 Five characters for occult use: wind, clouds, thunder, rain, and lightning (reading from top right). (From an undated Taoist work on exorcism, *Tao-tsang* 1152–40 : 18b)

32 Talisman to stop wind. (*Tao-tsang* 1152–41 : 30b)

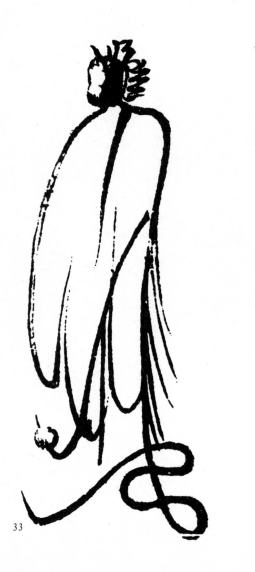

33

王女符

元亨利貞
合于冀

行遠六合不轉停

天地交泰
尠以神

三六四祐
伍玉司

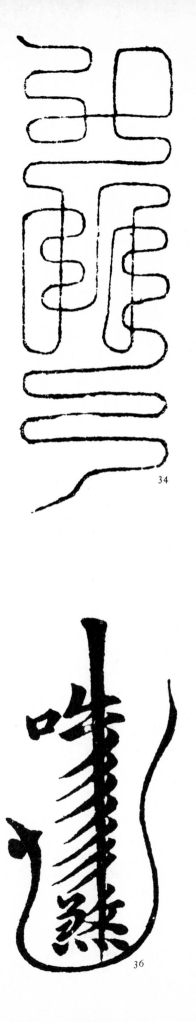

34

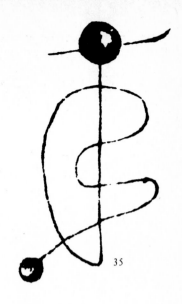

35

Protective talismans

34 Charm to protect against loss of voice. The centre part of the composition represents the lungs. (Early 12th century, *Tao-tsang* 463–267:6a)

35 Bird-headed talisman to protect the body and secure longevity. (From an undated Taoist work on exorcism, *Tao-tsang* 1152–43:9a)

36 Talisman to destroy evil influences and noxious spirits. The character *sheng* – 'life' – is mounted on a horse and penetrates through the character *sha* – 'to strike dead by evil influences'. (*Tao-tsang* 1152–35:10b)

37 Charm to protect all six kinds of domestic animals (i.e. oxen, sheep or goats, horses, pigs, dogs and fowls). (*Tao-tsang* 463–272:14b)

38 Talisman to protect status and salary. (*Tao-tsang* 463–272:13a)

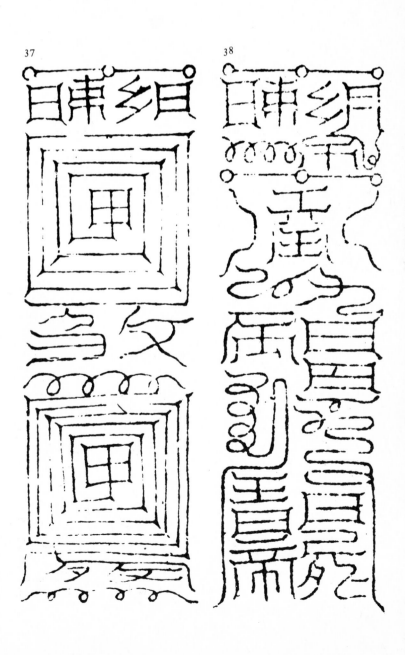

37

38

36

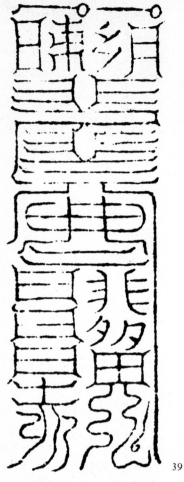

辟官災符

辟盗賊符

辟口舌符

39

39 Talisman to ward off male
visitors and guests. (Early 12th
century, *Tao-tsang* 463–272: 12b)

40 Charm to ward off robbers
and thieves. (*Tao-tsang*
463–272: 15a)

41 Talisman to protect against
wrangling. (*Tao-tsang* 463–272:
12b)

生 煞

40

生

41

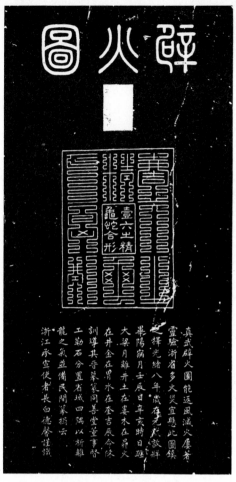

42

42 Diagram dated 1882 for warding off fire (centre) with a note: 'The Black Warrior's [Chen Wu's] Diagram for warding off fire possesses the property of repelling unpropitious winds and extinguishing fires and has on numerous occasions shown its miraculous power. The Province of Chekiang suffers greatly from fire: this may be avoided by hanging up a copy of this diagram [in your home]. I, Te Hsing, Prefect of Chekiang from the Mountain of Eternal Snow [in Manchuria], selected 9 p.m. on the 6th day of the 3rd moon of the 8th year of Kuang-hsü [AD 1882], the Year Star then being in the Dark, the Sign of the Month being in Pi [19th zodiacal constellation with the corresponding sign Moon], the Sun on its orbit having attained its nadir, and the Moon being in Ching [22nd zodiacal constellation], Saturn [Earth] in that of Lou [16th zodiacal constellation], Jupiter [Wood] in that of Mao [18th zodiacal constellation], Mars [Fire] in that of Ching [22nd zodical constellation], Venus [Metal] in that of Wei [17th zodiacal constellation], and Mercury [Water] in that of Kuei [15th zodiacal constellation]; as being an auspicious period in which to copy the Diagram. I accordingly instructed Chen Chi-chin, Sub-Director of Studies, to copy it, and assisted by the Director of the Hall of Authentic Texts, to supervise the engraving of it in stone, to be set up in the four corners of the cities of the Province to dispel malignant geomantic influences and to enable the people to procure rubbings.'

43 Two charms to protect against ghosts. (Tao-tsang 558–1:35b)

44 Two charms to protect the body from evil. (Tao-tsang 668–2:24a)

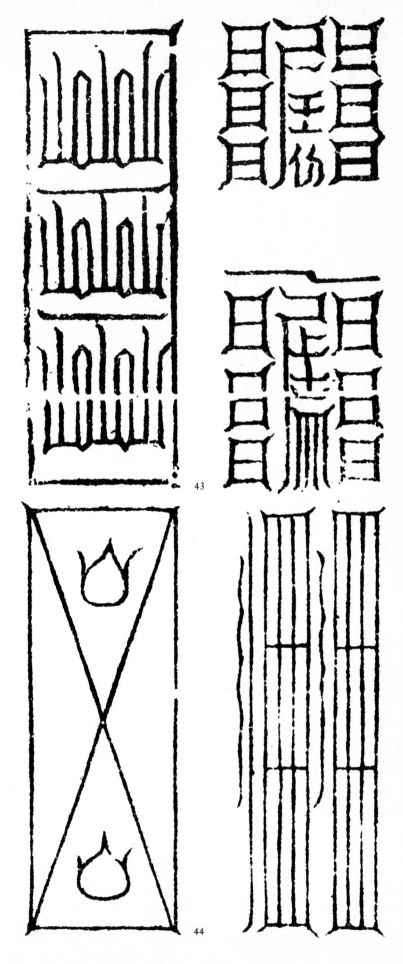

43

44

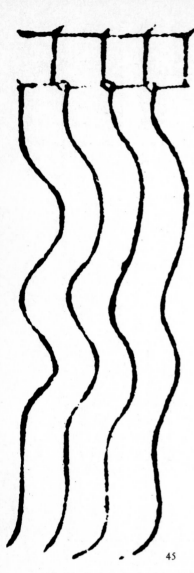

45

45 Good luck charm to give prolonged life; to be worn on belts. The design imitates a shamanistic belt. (From a Taoist work of unknown date, *Tao-tsang* 668–3:2a)

46 Charm to ease childbirth, incorporating the character *sheng* meaning 'to be born', 'life' and 'living'. (*Tao-tsang* 668–3:25b)

47 Charm to comfort the unborn child in the womb, incorporating constellation dots. (*Tao-tsang* 668–3: 21b)

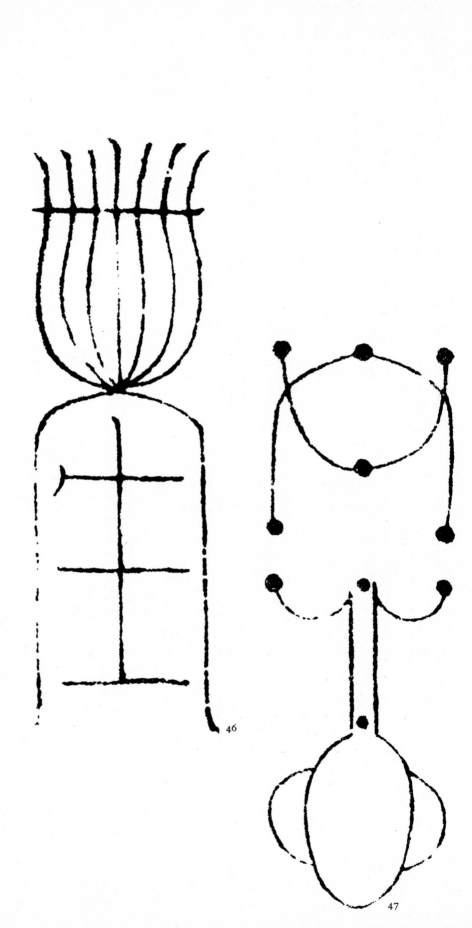

46

47

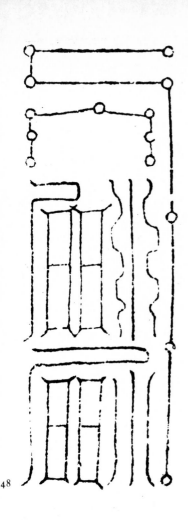

48

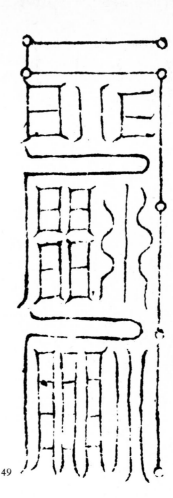

49

48 Talisman of the North. (Early 12th century, *Tao-tsang* 463–272:24b)

49 Talisman of the South. (*Tao-tsang* 463–272:24a)

50 Talisman of the Planet Mercury, the Star of Element Water. (*Tao-tsang* 463–271:29b)

51 Talisman of the Planet Venus, the Star of Element Metal. (*Tao-tsang* 463–271:29a)

52 Talisman of the Planet Jupiter, the Star of Element Wood. (*Tao-tsang* 463–271:28b)

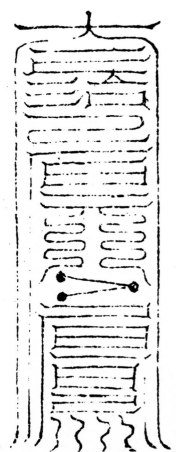

50

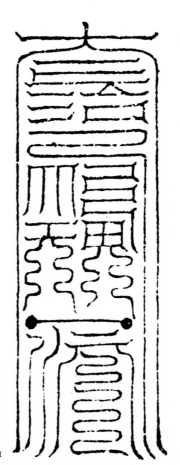

51

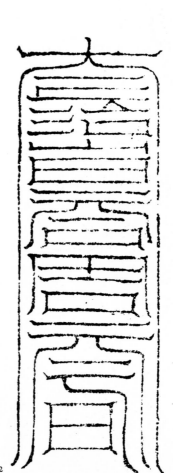

52

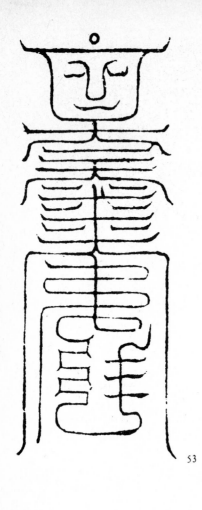

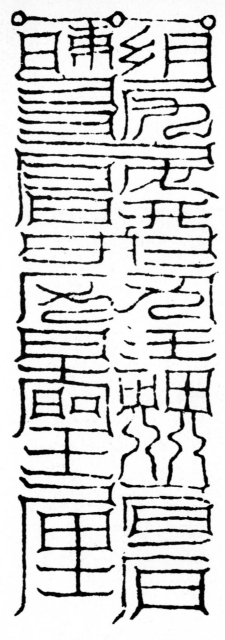

53

54

Curative talismans

53 Talisman to set a fractured skull. (*Tao-tsang* 543–35: 14b)

54 Charm to remove all diseases. (Early 12th-century, *Tao-tsang* 463–272: 14b)

55 Charm to set a fractured foot. (*Tao-tsang* 463–267: 5b)

56 Charm to improve vision. (*Tao-tsang* 463–267: 5b)

57 Charm against vomiting. (*Tao-tsang* 463–267: 6b)

58 Charm to remove deafness. (*Tao-tsang* 463–267: 6b)

續腳符

續目符

吐泥水符

開聾符

55

56

57

58

Implements of magic

59, 60 Magic divination table. The top is
decorated with dragons and phoenixes on a
background covered with esoteric diagrams to
guide the spirits to the centre. The design can
be related to the famous Yellow Book
Talisman (61). (19th century)

61 The Yellow Book Talisman. One of the
most powerful magic boards for contacting
spirits related to Earth. The format derives
from the square zone at the centre of the
ancient round bronze mirrors, considered to be
of great talismanic power. (*Tao-tsang*
1367–2a–3b)

60

61

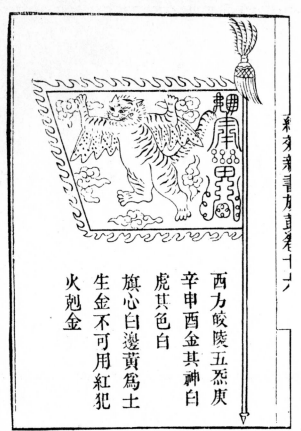

62

62 Banner with tiger and magic diagram. According to the Chinese caption, it belongs to 'the West, the White Mound, number 5, the 7th and 8th of the Ten Celestial Stems and the 9th and 10th of the Twelve Earthly Horary Branches and the Element Metal. Its spirit is the White Tiger and its colour is white. The centre of the banner is white and the border yellow, for Earth gives life to Metal. One cannot use red which offends Fire that destroys Metal.' (From a mid-16th-century work by Ch'i Shao-pao, *Chi-hsiao hsin-shu* 16:5b)

繪事備考旗軍卷十六

西方皎陵五烝庚
辛申酉金其神白
虎其色白
旗心白邊黃為土
生金不可用紅犯
火剋金

63

64 Example of the use of Taoist Cloud Script. (From the Yüan edition of *The Western Chamber* (*Hsi-hsiang chi*), 1:55a)

繪事備考旗軍卷十六

五行旗　金木水火土五面各照五行之色

此乃出征之旗代轉光旗之
用也桿用長鎗桿旗照字色可遠
本旗之色庶純而可遠
邊方紵五尺旗不用彩畫旗頭上
用白紵以字餘皆黑字旗頭
瞭用鎗頭便出征輕潔色純
不混眾目

63 Taoist banner of the Element Metal, one of a set of five for each of the Five Elements (Metal, Wood, Water, Fire and Earth) with their appropriate colours. (From a mid-16th-century work by Ch'i Shao-pao, *Chi-hsiao hsin-shu* 16:9b)

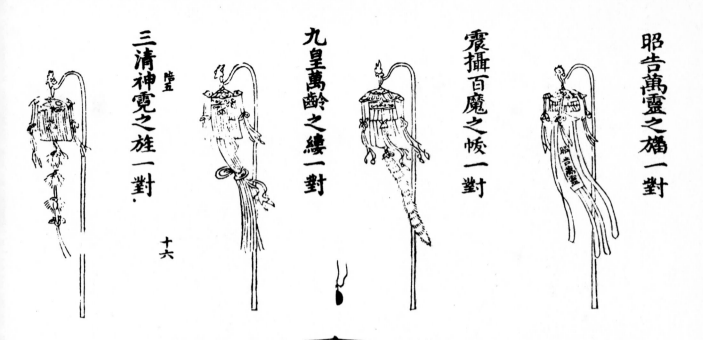

三清神霄之旌一對．

九皇萬齡之縷一對

震攝百魔之帳一對

昭告萬靈之旛一對

十六

65　Taoist implements of magical power.
Right to left: (i) the Pennant of the Ten
Thousand Spirits of the Luminous
Announcement; (ii) the Pennon of the
Hundred Malignant Spirits of Trembling
and Fear; (iii) the Threaded-banner of
Ten Thousand Years of Age of the Nine
Palaces; (iv) the Banner of the Rainbow of
the Spirits of the Three Pure Ones.
Tao-tsang 1460–5–19b:20a)

66　Right to left: (i) the Fan of the
Feathers of the Nine Heavens; (ii) the Fan
of the Clouds of Good Fortune of the
Fragrant Silk; (iii) the Umbrella of Rosy
Clouds of the Flying Spirits; (iv) the
Lantern of Light of the Partly Hidden
Candle. (*Tao-tsang* 1460–5:21b–22a)

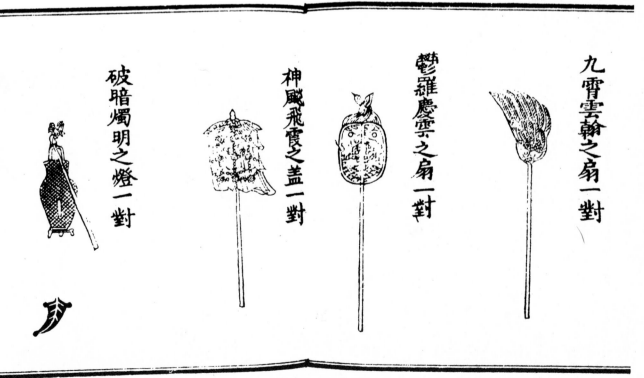

破暗燭明之燈一對

神威飛霞之蓋一對

鬱羅慶雲之扇一對

九霄雲翰之扇一對

67 Taoist magic sword carved out of peach-wood with rounded end, used symbolically as a sword against evil spirits and frequently employed as a writing instrument in talismanic calligraphy. The blade is decorated on one side with the figure of Lao-tzu (also known as Lao Chün or Lao Tan), commonly regarded as the originator of Taoism. He holds a scroll in one hand, and is riding under pine-trees on a water buffalo, on which, according to legend, he left China to travel towards the west. (19th century)

Note on the Tao-tsang (Taoist canon)

The first section (titles 1–313), the *Tung-chen* (Cave of Truth), contains documents of the Mao-shan Taoists, the highest ranking of all Taoist sects, with special knowledge of trances, spirit writing and meditation. The second section (314–614), the *Tung-hsüan* (Cave of Mystery), contains the powerful Five Talismans, texts of various liturgies, including the communal festival of Cosmic Renewal (*chiao*), and other talismans. The third section (615–975), the *Tung-shen* (Cave of Spirits), consists of the revelation given, at the end of the Eastern Han dynasty, to Chang Tao-ling, founder of the Heavenly Master Sect of Lung-shu-shan in Kiangsi Province. The fourth (976–1,086), fifth (1,087–1,152), and sixth (1,153–1,176) sections are described as supplements of the first, second, and third sections respectively; while the seventh section (1,177–1,412) is called *Cheng-i*, the 'Orthodox One'. A collection of later Taoist works (1,413–1,464) of various early Ming (post-Mongol) dates completes the edition. Diagrams and talismanic graphic illustrations appear throughout the whole canon. Source references in the captions of the present book are to title, chapter and page numbers (recto: a, verso: b), and are based on Wieger's index-numbers (see Bibliography).

Chronology

SHANG-YIN	BC c. 1600–1027
CHOU	1027– 221
CH'IN	221– 207
HAN	206– 220 (AD)
THREE KINGDOMS	221– 265
SIX DYNASTIES	265– 580
SUI	581– 618
T'ANG	618– 906
FIVE DYNASTIES	907– 960
SUNG	960–1279
YÜAN (MONGOLS)	1280–1368
MING	1368–1644
CH'ING (MANCHUS)	1644–1912
REPUBLIC	1912–1949
PEOPLE'S REPUBLIC	1949–

Bibliography

J. Blofeld, *The Secret and the Sublime*, London, 1973.
Cheng-t'ung Tao-tsang, Taoist canon, published under the Cheng-t'ung Emperor in 1436.
H. Doré, *Laotse et le Taoisme* (*Recherches sur les supersitions en Chine*, vol. 18), Shanghai, 1920.
J. J. M. de Groot, *The Religious System of China*, 6 vols, Leiden, 1892–1910.
I. L. Legeza, 'A new appraisal of Chün ware' in *Oriental Art*, n.s., vol. xvii, no. 3, Autumn 1972.
I. L. Legeza, 'Art and Tao' in *Apollo*, vol. xcv, no. 126, August 1972.
P. Rawson and L. Legeza, *Tao, The Chinese philosophy of time and change*, London, 1973.
M. R. Saso, *Taoism and the Rite of Cosmic Renewal*, Washington State University Press, 1972.
L. Wieger, *Taoisme*, 2 vols, n.p., 1911–13. (Index numbers used in the present book for individual works in the *Tao-tsang* are based on the Wieger numbers published in this work.)

Acknowledgments

Items illustrated are reproduced by courtesy of the following:
ARTIA, Prague 76, 77
Author's collection 40; fig 42
Chinese Literature (1967, no. 7)
Gulbenkian Museum, Durham p. 10, *pls*. 14, 20, 57, 70, 72, 76; fig. 69
S. Marchant & Sons, London 60
Private collections 24, 50; figs. 59–60
Sothebys & Co., London 13, 53, 68
University Library, Durham 17, 44, 45, 47
Wen-wu (1974, no. 9) 59
Photographs are by the following:
A. Hatton 41
China Pictorial (1968, no. 4) 71
Chinese Literature (1963, no. 7) 5
Wen-wu (1974, no. 9) 59
Jeff Teasdale, Durham, all others